LONDON'S
PARKS & GARDENS

LONDON'S PARKS & GARDENS

JILL BILLINGTON • PHOTOGRAPHS BY SANDRA LOUSADA

FRANCES LINCOLN

CONTENTS

For Sir Edward and Lady
Valerie Osmotherly, and my
indefatigable husband,
Bill Billington, who explored
many of the sites with me,
with such delight, whatever
the weather.
J.B.

This book is for Frances Lincoln,
whose idea it was.
S.L.

Frances Lincoln Ltd
4 Torriano Mews
Torriano Avenue
London NW5 2RZ
www.franceslincoln.com

London's Parks and Gardens
Copyright © Frances Lincoln Ltd 2003
Text copyright © Jill Billington 2003
Photographs copyright © Sandra Lousada 2003

First Frances Lincoln edition: 2003

A catalogue record for this book is available from
the British Library.

ISBN 0 7112 2039 5

Designed by Becky Clarke

Printed and bound in Singapore by Tien Wah Press

1 2 3 4 5 6 7 8 9

Right An eternally youthful Peter Pan stands in
Kensington Gardens, lonely but defiant.
Frontispiece The trees near the Serpentine Gallery
in Kensington Gardens on a wintry day when
snow replaces foliage.

Where to find London's parks and gardens

1	Bunhill Fields
2	Postman's Park
3	Barbican
4	No.1 Poultry
5	Broadgate Arena
6	St Paul's Churchyard
7	St Dunstan in the East
8	Canary Wharf
9	Island Gardens
10	University of East London
11	Thames Barrier Park
12	London Buddhist Centre
13	Victoria Park
14	Mile End Park
15	Geffrye Museum
16	Abney Park Cemetery
17	Lincoln's Inn Fields
18	Gray's Inn
19	The Middle and Inner Temples
20	Russell Square
21	Bloomsbury Square
22	Fitzroy Square
23	British Library
24	Calthorpe Project Community Garden
25	New River Walk
26	Malvern Terrace
27	Culpeper Community Gardens
28	Camley Street Natural Park
29	Cross Club
30	Myddelton House
31	Forty Hall
32	Hilly Fields
33	Grovelands Park
34	Capel Manor
35	Lea Valley Regional Park
36	Epping Forest
37	Wanstead Park
38	Hainault Forest
39	Berkeley Square
40	Grosvenor Square
41	Mount Street Gardens
42	St James's Park
43	Green Park
44	Victoria Embankment Gardens
45	Victoria Tower Gardens
46	Westminster Abbey
47	Chester Square
48	Eccleston Square
49	Chelsea Physic Garden
50	Chelsea Royal Hospital
51	Fulham Palace
52	The River Café
53	Regent's Park
54	Primrose Hill
55	Hampstead Heath
56	Parliament Hill Fields
57	Golders Hill Park
58	The Hill
59	Fenton House
60	Kenwood House
61	Waterlow Park and Lauderdale House
62	Highgate Cemetery
63	Highgate and Queen's Woods
64	Alexandra Palace
65	Avenue House Arboretum
66	Hyde Park
67	Kensington Gardens
68	The Roof Garden
69	Holland Park
70	Victoria and Albert Museum and Natural History Museum
71	Emslie Horniman Pleasance
72	Meanwhile Gardens
73	Little Venice
74	Clifton Nurseries
75	Chiswick House
76	Chiswick Mall
77	Syon House
78	Osterley Park
79	Gunnersbury Park
80	Gunnersbury Triangle Ecological Park
81	Royal Botanic Gardens
82	Marble Hill House
83	York House
84	Hampton Court Palace
85	Bushy Park
86	Richmond Park
87	Ham House
88	Barnes Wildfowl and Wetlands Trust
89	Museum of Garden History
90	Bonnington Square
91	Roots and Shoots Nursery
92	Brockwell Park
93	Burgess Park and Chumleigh Multicultural Gardens
94	Greenwich Park.
95	Blackheath
96	Crystal Palace Park
97	Dulwich Park
98	Lesnes Abbey Woods
99	Oxleas Wood
100	Maryon Park and Maryon Wilson Park
101	Peckham Rye Park
102	Choumert Square
103	Horniman Museum
104	Eltham Palace
105	Hall Place
106	Beckenham Place Park
107	Battersea Park
108	Wimbledon Common
109	Cannizaro Park

W7
W13
W5
79
78
77
81
ISLEWORTH
83 82
87
86
85
84
HAMPTON WICK

Introduction

Much of London's special character stems from the open spaces within it. Over centuries, despite regular threats of enclosure and urbanization, London has managed to retain, create and develop green areas in large sweeps and small pockets – sometimes flushed with flowers or studded with splendid trees, sometimes wild, sometimes made magnificent by the hand of man; sometimes open and spacious, sometimes hidden. These areas include royal parks, old estates, deer parks, the grounds of country houses, commons, heaths, nature reserves, community gardens, private gardens, botanical gardens, garden squares, cemeteries and municipal parks. Altogether the city can claim to have over 67 square miles of open space, among which are 1,700 spaces that are over 1 acre in size. A large proportion of these are accessible to the public. Few cities of the world provide as much open space for nature and people as is found in London.

That there are so many parks and gardens for the public to enjoy today is thanks to the efforts of public authorities and private individuals. Many historic places have been under threat in the past and were saved for public use; others have been created anew in recent times.

We owe many of our parks and gardens to the monarchy who, in preserving large tracts of land for their own pleasure, became in effect the protectors of green London. Though the property of the reigning monarch, the royal parks have long been openly available to the people. (It is said that when Queen Caroline, consort of George II, asked Sir Robert Walpole what it would cost to enclose Kensington Gardens for herself, she received the reply, 'Your Crowns, Ma'am.') Since 1851, when the Crown officially handed over the administration of the royal parks to the Government they have been publicly funded.

They are now managed by the Royal Parks Agency.

In London as all over England, the people lost much common land to enclosure by landowners who claimed the land as private property. People saw not only their precious countryside taken away from them but also their commoners' rights to obtain food and firewood. It was a milestone when, in 1866, the Metropolitan Commons Act put a stop to further enclosures.

Another turning point in the story of London's green places also came in Victorian times when it was recognized that nature and green spaces played a part in improving physical health and spiritual well-being. In 1833 the Select Committee on Public Works reported on the few areas as yet undeveloped, in particular wasteland in east London and areas on the south bank of the Thames, where it would have been all too easy to build yet more cramped terraces. The subsequent setting aside of land for urban communities was one of the great contributions of the Victorians to society.

The future of green places became more secure when public bodies began to assume responsibility for public parks and gardens. The Corporation of London started annexing land for public recreation in 1878, collecting under its wing, for example, Epping Forest and Highgate Wood. In the twentieth century, the Greater London Council took on Hampstead Heath, Trent Park, Holland Park, Crystal Palace and others. The National Trust, estab-lished in 1895, has been effective in ensuring the security of open places, and the public owe their access to a number of gardens in London to the work of the Trust. Organizations such as the Victorian Society and the Georgian Group have also been influential in saving buildings and their associated gardens.

Individual visionaries have campaigned for green spaces in

London, and continue to do so. Just as in the nineteenth century Thomas Willingdale fought for Epping Forest, recently the architect Lord Rogers put forward a strong case – now on the agenda of the Greater London Authority – for linking the royal parks with a green route along the River Thames and putting the car second to nature by sending it underground. Likewise groups of individuals, organized as Friends of a particular place, have been instrumental in saving parks and gardens from closure or neglect.

In 1938 the outer London local authorities decided that a protected area around the perimeter was necessary and established the Green Belt. By restricting building development in an area of connecting farmland, public commons, purchased estate land and wild woodlands encircling expanding suburbia, it saved many green spaces on the outskirts of London for public enjoyment.

The Second World War left many parks and gardens in need of extensive repair, as they had served the nation by being dug for victory and used for military purposes. But the bombing created opportunities to develop new green places in devastated areas where once there had been buildings. Post-war development was also influenced by the County of London Plan and the Greater London Plan, prepared by the planner Lord Abercrombie. These aimed to balance density of housing with the provision of open space, and to create an improved London with 'green lungs' that had not just 'order and efficiency' but essentially 'beauty and spaciousness'. After the end of the war such planning was expanded to include severely bomb-damaged areas.

In the twenty-first century it is the Government's declared intention to reaffirm the importance of urban parks as 'places for people'. It recently created an Urban Green Spaces Taskforce, which has recommended setting up an agency dedicated to this end. The well-being of urban people remains a priority for local authorities. Many of the London boroughs are trying to increase spending on their open spaces, while the Greater London Authority is committed to an 'urban renaissance in London' and the draft London Plan outlines future proposals, including ways to green the city. The London Development Agency, Transport for London and the Architecture and Urbanism Unit are all involved in the London Plan. Diverse pilot projects have been identified – including plans to improve and green the heart of neighbourhoods like Brixton Central Square and to safeguard natural areas like Rainham Marshes – and work has started in some places.

Other agencies have vigorously taken on derelict areas. Increasingly, the desire to conserve nature in towns has rescued many sites. The London Ecology Unit and the London Wildlife Trust sustain many such places; some of these areas have become registered as Sites of Special Scientific Interest, protecting them from development. Other nature reserves can be found all over London. Functioning waterways have had their associated marshes set aside so as to maintain natural biodiversity.

Sometimes abandoned spaces have been saved to make gardens for communities. These often involve active local participation, introducing adults and schools to conservation as well as to horticulture. They can also become important places for binding neighbours together. Other developments of recent decades include walkways such as the London Loop, which offers a linked green walk around outer London. Ultimately the London Walkers' Web will link many existing green parts of the metropolis. Other routes follow the 'green lungs' of the canals that penetrate the urban heart of London. Cemeteries, too, have become valued havens of nature. Despite the urbanization of the modern world, London's green spaces flourish.

Today new designers are taking up the baton from past distinguished garden architects – including Humphry Repton,

William Kent, Lancelot 'Capability' Brown – associated with London's parks. Formal bedding is still popular, but there are also examples of contemporary 'naturalistic' styles, and, in contrast, the exotic semitropical planting favoured by London's increasingly mild climate. In recent years, the notion of the garden has expanded. With the growing interest in ecological balance and an increasing passion for urban wildlife, the casual look of well-managed wildlife gardens is now appealing to city dwellers and many public parks have such areas.

But providing for everyone's needs and preferences is not easy and the labour necessary for parks and gardens is costly. Even 'wild' areas such as the marshes and gravel pits of Barnes wetlands are expensive, requiring expert management. Where restoration projects have been initiated money is required not only for the restoration itself but also for subsequent maintenance. Frequently it is local authorities that bear the financial burdens, and they are striving to address the problems in various ways, including working together to spread the load. Sponsorship and grants are becoming essential, the Heritage Lottery Fund being a source for many projects. Sharing gardens by opening them to the public is another way of helping to fund upkeep.

One of the most rewarding discoveries I have made in the course of writing this book is how generous people are. In the past land has been given to the public by philanthropic landowners. Today, people continue to give not just their money but, equally precious, their time, not only to save places but also to help maintain them. Many volunteer groups are devoted to their local sites and authorities and conservation organizations often depend on the efforts and expertise of volunteers. Many projects demand a considerable amount of time and money, but having seen the will and the energy that are devoted to them, I feel confident that the future for them, and for London's parks and gardens in general, looks good.

In this book I have been able to explore no more than a cross-section of parks and gardens. Had I included all the places I would have liked to describe, the book would have been too heavy to lift and, regrettably, I have had to omit some very fine ones. There are brief details of some of these on pages 234–5.

All the gardens mentioned in the book are open to the public, but you should check opening times before visiting. Many can be visited under the Yellow Book or National Gardens Scheme, by which owners welcome visitors to their private gardens on specified days. And on London Garden Squares Day in June many private squares are open to the public, an opportunity not to be missed. For details of these schemes, which include many more gardens than those here, and how to find out about the opening times of other gardens in this book, see page 236.

Sandra Lousada and I have taken huge pleasure in exploring the variety of London's green spaces. The experience of each place is totally individual. A wonderful aspects of gardens is that nature takes its course: no matter how we controlling humans try to ensure our input for eternity, nature will ultimately have a stronger say; the only thing that gardens can be relied upon to do is to change. Added to this, light alters everything by the hour, by the day and by the season. The one constant in London's open spaces is the green of the living ingredients that soften urban harshness, pulling together the muddle of the city.

It has been a delight also to see how important these spaces are for people, both the people of London and visitors to the city. I hope that this book will help you too to discover the rich and various pleasures of London's open spaces for yourself.

Top left The Gray's Inn Road entrance to the Calthorpe Community Gardens.
Top right Tiles commemorating little-known heroes at Postman's Park.
Centre left Immaculate borders at Hall Place.
Centre right The tube train rattles past cow parsley in the wildlife gardens of Gunnersbury Triangle Ecological Park.
Bottom Autumn colour in Kensington Gardens.

ANCIENT AND MODERN

THE CITY, DOCKLANDS AND THE EAST END

with green. They front one of the most open, windswept sites that London has to offer, facing the ruffled surface of the long dock and the runway of the City Airport. They contrast with the

Above left Christopher Wren's 'best view' of Greenwich, from Island Gardens on the Isle of Dogs.
Above right Windy open spaciousness with sculptural architecture characterizes the site of the University of East London.

enclosed but airy geometry of the main university building with its slim steel structural piers and a white-surfaced linear design. Subtle use of paint on parts of the buildings and the warm 'Minoan' red of the entrance façade add warmth and a note of invitation to the site.

The landscaping here is simple and geometric, like the raised platform that is University Square, which has a wide accessible

ramp suggesting many different functions. Beside the twinned student blocks are parabolic lawns with curves that echo the drum-like buildings. These grassed areas are edged by two-tiered wide black engineering bricks, which make a continuous bench seat for summer days. The views are splendidly light and spacious. Nevertheless this exciting place, designed by the architects Cullinans, has a freshness that responds to its youthful connections while also catching the atmosphere of the cleared site. A planned development promises to be as pleasing as that already available. It is easily accessible from the City by the elevated Docklands Light Railway.

THAMES BARRIER PARK
E16

On the north side of the river, below Canary Wharf, there used to be very little green. Bleak disused docklands and the contaminated industrial land of east London were sorely in need of regeneration. But then in 1982 the remarkable Thames Flood Barrier was built, as a defence against high tides that might otherwise have drowned London. A marvel of engineering that is also a series of magnificent shining steel sculptural pieces stretching across the river, the barrier became a powerful new focus and prompted the redevelopment of sites on both banks. As part of a master plan that included the ill-fated Dome on the south side, a bold new park was proposed for the north bank.

Thames Barrier Park is one of the few really modern London parks, and the first new riverside park to be opened in London for fifty years. The immediate objective was to regenerate the contaminated former petrochemical site. This was covered and sealed to form a levelled green plateau, which transformed the

Left Looking along the Green Dock that cleaves through the flat plain of Thames Barrier Park.
Right The metallic silver humps of the Barrier provide a focus for the park.

site into a suitable and delightful place for the local community. The *raison d'être* for the design of the park comes from the docks and the river, but the huge silver abstracts of the Barrier provide the focus. The new park had to be contemporary in its design; the traditional decorative Victorian style of London parks would not have been appropriate when the view is so dramatically modern. As a result of a competition, a plan was chosen that was based upon Anglo-French co-operation. The designer Alain Provost of Group Signes headed a team that included the urban designers Patel Taylor and engineers Ove Arup and Partners. The concept can be compared with the restructuring of the former Citroën site in Paris, Parc André Citroën, also designed by Alain Provost, and the layout shares some characteristics. It is powerfully linear and directional, drawing the visitor to the River Thames and the superb sculptural forms of the Barrier.

The core of the plan is a large grassed plateau, on a level with the embankment beside the river, but cutting through this is a sunken long rectangular channel, 13 feet/4 metres deep, that follows the line of the original Royal Docks directly towards the gleaming humps of the barrier. Now the floor of the channel is greened with plants and the long battered high walls on either side are blanketed with *Lonicera nitida* 'Maigrün', an easily clipped evergreen. This is the Green Dock, a ghost of its predecessor. Deep in the chasm, parallel rolling waves of yew hedges, with narrow paths between them, reinforce the original underlying order and reflect the energy of the river. The resulting microclimate protects lush blocks of plants, including herbaceous perennials, flowering shrubs and ornamental grasses. Such rich detail contrasts dramatically in texture and colour with the plainer green spaces above.

The main road end of the Green Dock culminates in a concrete and marble courtyard, bereft of plants but animated by thirty-six water jets. These spurt in computer-controlled sequence, amusing families and tempting children on bicycles. The other end climaxes in rolling grassland cut through by a concreted ravine and leading to a spacious timber deck overlooking the river. Here a dominating Pavilion of Remembrance, 25 feet/7.5 metres high, is dedicated to local people who died during the two world wars. A wide promenade runs along the riverbank, with magnificent views of the Barrier and towards the City of London.

The rest of the site is still growing, with longitudinal grids of birches, sweet gum (*Liquidambar styraciflua*), black pine (*Pinus nigra*), Norway maples (*Acer platanoides*), Japanese pagoda trees (*Sophora japonica*), American honey locust trees (*Gleditsia triacanthos*) and Hungarian oaks (*Quercus frainetto*). Straight paths cut through, some of them bridging the dock. There are also sports facilities, a wildlife area and a children's playground. The park will take some time to mature, but it is already remarkable.

LONDON BUDDHIST CENTRE
E2

All over London there are tiny flower-filled gardens that people have made in courtyards behind Georgian and Victorian terraced houses. But this one has a distinctly spiritual feeling. On entering, the visitor faces an intimate, timber-covered arbour, a shrine with a small stone-carved fountain, where three tiers of small troughs quietly fill and seep with clear water. Beside this, a seat invites you to pause, to contemplate and to enjoy the stirring of the senses as you catch the gentle sound of the water, breathe in the fragrant atmosphere created by herbs, aromatic foliage and scented flowers, and gaze at a surprising selection of plants, all well cared for in containers.

On the walls are climbing shrubs such as evergreen Californian lilac, with roses and a passion flower. A sense of seclusion is achieved with side curtains of evergreen bamboo, camellias and pittosporum. In the containers there are white and pink camellias, blue *Omphalodes verna*, small narcissi and deep-red tree peonies for spring. Lilac-pink evergreen hebes contrast with fresh green acers, and there are hydrangeas for autumn. Overhead on the arch are climbing roses, clematis and blue-flowering *Solanum crispum* 'Glasnevin'. Look higher up and you see an exquisite mural of lotus flowers painted on the wall facing the entrance. There is also a glass and metal design over the double doors, the crest of Nelanda University in India.

As well as this small courtyard, which is open every day, there are many little gardens on different levels, reached by steps that take visitors to every floor level. These are mostly private, but visitors are welcomed on open days. These tiny roof spaces are brimming with plants in containers. In summer there are the glorious colours of petunias, nasturtiums, lilies and pelargoniums, backed by small flowering shrubs such as potentillas, fuchsias and hydrangeas in larger tubs. Ornamental grasses, ferns and trailing ivies add texture.

VICTORIA PARK
E9

Victoria Park in Bethnal Green was the first public park to be made in London. By the middle of the eighteenth century this part of the East End was densely populated by silk weavers and dyers, overflowing from Spitalfields; a hundred years later, in Victorian times, the overcrowding and poverty had become acute. Living conditions were appalling: there was no sanitation, the air was polluted and there was little prospect of improvement. The ill health that burgeoned in such conditions was a threat not only to the poor but to the whole of society. Various measures were proposed to relieve the situation, and among them was the suggestion that a green open space should be created.

Right The tiny, intimate and tranquil courtyard of the London Buddhist Centre is backed by a high wall painting of lotus flowers.

As a result of a petition to the Queen and an Act of Parliament, an area of 290 acres, including Bonner's Fields and the site of the manor house of Stepney, was purchased by the Crown. Named Victoria Park for the Queen, it was laid out in the 1840s as a park for the people. The plan was drawn up by Sir James Pennethorne, a protégé of the architect John Nash. Pennethorne found the site flat and uninteresting, but planted 40,000 trees and shrubs, and had lakes excavated, one of them a boating lake with an arcade attached. A song of the day tells how:

The Park is called the People's Park
And all the walks are theirs,
And strolling through the flowery paths
They breathe exotic Airs …

Above Victoria Park's tall fountain mists the lake on a windy day, as children play near by.

The park became a focus for political activity, including the Chartists' demonstrations in 1848. William Morris and later Bernard Shaw were among the speakers who used Victoria Park as a platform to press for social reform.

Today the park is split in two by Grove Road and the two areas are quite distinct in character. One is a large flat open space, bordered by the Grand Union Canal and the Hertford Union Canal, with old iron bridges including Three Colts Bridge. Attractive canal-side walks link to the Bow Heritage Trail. The open area has many pitches for football, rugby, cricket and a bowling green, but it is children who animate it: there is a playground with undulating scope for adventures, and an animal enclosure close by. An open-air theatre and a café sustain mind and body. Embellishments include an elegant bandstand as well as an elaborate memorial drinking fountain of 1861, donated by the philanthropic Angela Burdett-Coutts.

Beside one of the lakes a wild area provides a habitat for squirrels and other small animals, and there is an enclosed Old English Garden, which has fragrant and flowering shrubs including lilac, lavender and roses, with perennials and summer bedding providing colour. There are many large trees including fine horse chestnuts and rows of planes by the canal, plus some more unusual specimens such as the white-flowering Chinese privet (*Ligustrum lucidum*), Caucasian lime (*Tilia dasystyla*) and Kentucky coffee tree (*Gymnocladus dioica*).

The other, smaller and more intimate section of Victoria Park has a large lake and a small hilly terrain that is fun to walk through. In the centre of the lake a high spurting fountain sprays randomly in the wind. Surrounding shrub borders planted for year-round interest include amelanchiers, fuchsias, phormiums, spireas, cortaderia and brachyglottis. There are also formal beds that are brilliantly planted for spring and summer. The rather shabby rockery, too tempting for small feet to explore, has large pieces of water-worn limestone and is in need of replacing.

MILE END PARK
E1 and E2

West of Victoria Park and connected to it by the Regent's Canal is a narrow strip of green space that is Mile End Park – about a mile long and at most only half a mile wide, narrowing to considerably less in several places. Originally created in 1943 as part of the wartime County of London Plan, when the regeneration of a derelict brownfield site offered a linear green routeway to the river at Limehouse, it is now being extended following an exciting contemporary design to serve the locality. As yet it is separated from Victoria Park by buildings and roads, but the aim is to create a green route for pedestrians to follow the thread of the canal.

This area of Stepney has a tradition of social service: it was here that in 1868 William Booth established the Salvation Army and in 1870 the first of Dr Barnardo's orphanages was founded. The Blitz of the Second World War caused much devastation, but now the area is revitalized.

The principle of regenerating the area by greening it was a strong influence in the design of the park. An Ecology Park is being built and there are earth mounds creating a hilly terrain. Even the noisy channel that is the Mile End Road is crossed by greenery: the popular Green Bridge, designed by Piers Gough, is a wide grassed pedestrian walkway and cycle route that allows no interruption between the two areas of green parkland on either side. Based upon a concrete deck, the bridge arches smoothly over the road. The structure is composed of a layer of lightweight polystyrene laid over a concrete base, and geo-textile that holds enough planting medium to support grassed areas, with several tree groups, on either side of the path. The trees are large multi-stemmed Himalayan birches (*Betula utilis* var. *jacquemontii*), whose characteristic graphic white trunks make them perfect companions for the evergreen black pines (*Pinus nigra*) and contrasting finer, more silvery, Weymouth pines (*P. strobus*).

From the crest of the bridge there is a view towards Limehouse and the towers of Canary Wharf. Wandering over the gentle rise of the bridge the visitor is unaware of the cheerful yellow soffit beneath. The arch of the bridge has been designed to include a convex cross-section that allows light to flood the road below.

To the south of the bridge is a gentle terraced garden that curves around a large pool, fed by wide weirs from another smaller area of water. Flowering shrubs, roses, perennials and ornamental grasses provide softening textures and colours for most of the year, and many contemporary but comfortable seats are provided at every level. Across from the terraces some large rocks are casually but effectively placed to appear natural.

The north side of the bridge, which leads eventually to the Ecology Park, is quite different in spirit. Here the intention is to create an arts park. Again it is set with a flat reflective pool of water, but this one is geometrically hard-edged and a high walk swerves around it, bounded by tall curved ribs of timber, reminiscent of the structure of a boat. There is an events building, which is partially concealed with earth to comply with the desire for green open land in this part of east London. This high-tech building is designed to use 'annual passive heat store technology', which means that about a 20 feet/6 metres depth of soil around the building is dry and stores summer heat, sufficient to warm the structure in winter.

There is also a children's area with an earth mound, so all needs are catered for. Regrettably, maintenance (and vandalism) are always problems in urban parks, and the early enthusiasm for building a new environment can be sadly missing when it comes to supporting it over the years. This scheme, however, has a ten-year maintenance programme and includes the building of some features to earn money to pay for

Left Bold contemporary design is the keynote of Mile End Park.

upkeep. The Green Bridge provides income from nine shop units below that front the Mile End Road. And the glass-fronted arts and technology building will draw paying visitors when it is complete. Making parks self-financing in this way is part of a solution to quality of upkeep and crucial to their success.

The Victorian ideal, as evidenced in Victoria Park, of providing pleasant open space in a deprived area, is revived here. This 'people's park fit for the 21st century' will eventually provide activities for all ages, including sports, the arts, playgrounds, gardens and nature areas, ensuring its continued popularity. This was emphasized in the proposals for the park put to the Millennium Commission by the local environment agency, Community Land Use. The Mile End Partnership has now been formed to collaborate with other local agencies to manage the project.

GEFFRYE MUSEUM
E2

In 1714, under the bequest of Sir Robert Geffrye, master of the Ironmongers' Company and Lord Mayor of London, some charming almshouses were built at Kingsland Road. At the time the surrounding land was farmed as market gardens to supply the City with vegetables and herbs. But in the early part of Queen Victoria's reign, the surroundings, having become densely overpopulated by the poor, were heavily built-up and unsanitary. The buildings were sold to the London County Council in 1910 and by 1914 had been converted to its current use as a museum – fostered initially by the Arts and Crafts Movement and now run by a trust – specializing in English domestic interiors of the urban middle classes. It also provides an oasis of green calm amidst the chaos of urban life.

Influenced by the London tradition of attaching small personal plots to homes however humble, the museum has

– all plants that had been brought to England from the New World. The great plant hunters of the nineteenth century are represented in the High Victorian Garden, with tender perennials and a greenhouse in which to overwinter them. Brightly coloured annual carpet bedding, ferns, dahlias and pelargoniums are set amongst an evergreen shrubbery.

Linked to this is the Edwardian Garden, which has a central circular pool and a typical simple timber pergola on brick piers, covered with clematis, wisteria and hybrid climbing roses. These are enhanced with summer-long herbaceous flowers backed by abutilon and ceanothus on the walls. Plants and herbs of the past came back into fashion in Edwardian times, and the garden also includes columbine, candytuft, hollyhocks, pinks and lilies mixing with mullein, sage, artemisia, rosemary, lavender and santolina.

The front garden is formal, now mostly lawn surrounded by tall London plane trees.

ABNEY PARK CEMETERY
N16

This wonderfully overgrown Victorian cemetery in Stamford Hill, north London, is neglected but not unloved. A trust is working with the local authority of Hackney to preserve the status quo, as opposed to tidying and cleaning the site, because unintentionally it has become a nature reserve. The thick undergrowth of bluebells, cow parsley, brambles and pink willow herb covers and almost hides many of the smaller tombstones. Such density, built up over a long period, has established an ecological balance, creating habitats for flora and fauna that are more likely to be associated with deep countryside, far beyond London's boundaries.

Above Christmas at the Geffrye Museum is celebrated in all the period rooms – each with its own appropriate seasonal decoration – and outside as well.

created behind the almshouses a series of attractive small period gardens that illustrate the changes in fashion of the domestic garden.

The Knot Garden in the style of 1550 has a decorative pattern of coloured gravels filling in beds of interwoven cotton lavender (*Santolina chamaecyparissus*) and germander (*Teucrium chamaedrys*). The Elizabethan Garden features the herbs for health, hygiene and food that were a major part of gardens of that time, including bay, chamomile, chives, fennel, lovage, rosemary and thyme, along with pear, hawthorn and old roses. The design is simple and geometric, with raised beds, to suit the functional intention of the garden.

The third garden shows how in the Regency fashion took over from function: the design is more elegant, hedged and edged with clipped holly, box, laurel, privet and yew to establish formality. The symmetrical beds are filled with irises, lilies and peonies, with some areas reserved for roses. With these grow fig, lilac, hibiscus, honeysuckle and Virginia creeper

The cemetery covers an area of 30 acres. Like many of the Victorian cemeteries, it was opened because many of the old small burial grounds were crammed full and becoming a health hazard. In this case one was needed to cope with the overflow from Bunhill Fields – specifically there was a need for unconsecrated ground suitable for burying Dissenters. The grounds of the Manor of Stoke Newington, owned by Sir Thomas Abney, Mayor of London in 1700, seemed ideal, as he had been a leading Nonconformist. The site was opened for business in 1840 and dramatic architecture, which included a neogothic chapel, Egyptian Revival lodges and a neoclassical mausoleum, set a theatrical style. Some more recent and simpler tombstones include those of William Booth, founder of the Salvation Army.

The finest feature of Abney Park is the tree collection. The founding editor of the *Gardener's Magazine*, J.C. Loudon, described it in the 1840s as 'one of the most complete arboretums in the neighbourhood of London'. At that time all the trees were labelled. There are still huge old horse chestnuts, sycamores and willows from then and blossoming hawthorns, rowans, crab apples and cherries. The cemetery is a peaceful place, albeit surrounded by teeming traffic on three sides. Birds sing in the canopy, and small animals can be heard in the undergrowth. Scrambling trailing plants attempt to conceal every feature and follow the inclining trees and tombstones that were once vertical. The atmosphere is that of a romantic wilderness scene from a grand opera, in which some of the graves are major soloists while others are touchingly ranked in the parallel lines of the chorus.

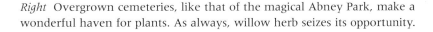
Right Overgrown cemeteries, like that of the magical Abney Park, make a wonderful haven for plants. As always, willow herb seizes its opportunity.

ORDER AND THE COMMUNITY

THE INNS OF COURT, BLOOMSBURY, KING'S CROSS AND ISLINGTON

ORDER AND THE COMMUNITY
The Inns of Court, Bloomsbury,
King's Cross and Islington

Lincoln's Inn Fields, Gray's Inn, The Middle and Inner Temples, Russell Square, Bloomsbury Square and Fitzroy Square,
British Library, Calthorpe Project Community Garden, New River Walk, Malvern Terrace,
Culpeper Community Gardens, Camley Street Natural Park, Cross Club

Discreetly hidden between the ancient City and Westminster, leading northwards from the River Thames, are the four great Inns of Court, established around Chancery Lane in the fourteenth century for the purpose of teaching the law. This is legal London, where today fully fledged barristers practise. Largely planned upon the style of Oxford and Cambridge colleges, the inns have associated gardens and benefit from the open space of Lincoln's Inn Fields near by.

Further north are some of London's famous squares, built as London expanded westwards from the overcrowded City. From the seventeenth century wealthy families bought up land to build themselves large houses. They were followed by speculators who took advantage of the new opportunities. By the nineteenth century most of the aristocrats' mansions had been replaced by graciously proportioned terraces set around a central area. Typical of these are Russell, Bloomsbury and Fitzroy Squares. At first not all squares were enclosed: some were laid out on geometric principles, some represented wilderness and others were used for grazing; later some were made into gardens. Today most are still in their different ways places of refreshing greenery, giving London much of its unique character. Near by, the new piazza of the British Library provides an open space of quite a different kind.

Once part of the great forest of Middlesex, by the sixteenth century Islington was known for its handsome mansions with gardens and orchards. Henry VIII found it handy for hunting and other more secret pleasures. Being outside the City it became a refuge in times of plague and also for troubled dissenters. But although in the eighteenth century Islington was still green, with grazing lands that kept London supplied with milk, gradually the streets became lined with densely packed rows of flat-fronted Georgian and Regency houses. Few of their front gardens survived development into shops – Malvern Terrace being an exception – and council estates filled up what spaces were left. However, local people have taken the problem of lack of gardens into their own hands. The Islington, Bloomsbury and King's Cross area includes several community gardens, such as the Culpeper Community Gardens, whose existence is due to the imagination and persistence of the few for the many. Another saviour of this part of London is the New River Walk, whose leafy path provides an oasis in this built-up area.

LINCOLN'S INN FIELDS
WC2

The 7 acres of green space here survive from common grazing land. An area notorious for thieves and beggars, who were attracted by the popular sideshows of fairs held there, it was enclosed in the seventeenth century. It subsequently survived many attempted incursions by developers, initially because it was protected by James I and later because of its powerful associations with the Law Courts, and the main part was retained as an open space. Today Lincoln's Inn Fields is one of the largest areas of green space in the City. Lawyers' chambers frame the square, which is ringed with a circulatory path and divided into four by crossing paths that meet at a bandstand.

Huge old plane trees, mulberries and writhing wisteria indicate the age of the garden. Other items of horticultural interest include the recently built rockery and a thriving collection of subtropical plants. Alongside agaves are tree ferns (*Dicksonia antarctica*), bushy fan palms (*Chamaerops humilis*), honey spurge (*Euphorbia mellifera*) and the dead-looking toothed lancewood (*Pseudopanax ferox*). The exotic look is eked out during winter by hardier but nevertheless exotic-looking large spiny yuccas, palmate fatsias, bamboos and pampas grasses.

There is also a dry sunny area, where plants have been selected to survive without irrigation. Here are brown-leaved sedges and grasses, with spring bulbs among a few carefully placed rocks, all overseen by wide-spreading flowering cherry trees.

To the north of the square is the eclectic museum of the collector Sir John Soane. This is crammed with architectural fragments, prints and paintings, displayed as they were in Soane's own time. Opposite, on the south side of the square, and catering for quite different historical enthusiasms, is another museum, that of the Royal College of Surgeons.

Pages 38–39 Looking through Brewster Gates to the elegantly collegiate New Square in Lincoln's Inn.
Page 41 Huge trees cast shadows on the sweeping grass below the terraced walk of Gray's Inn.
Above left Reflected sunlight reveals the tracery in the roof of the open cloisters beside the Old Square of Gray's Inn.
Above right Ancient trees spread widely on Lincoln's Inn Fields.

Crossing the road on the east side you arrive at Lincoln's Inn. Founded in the fourteenth century, the Inn is a series of fine buildings with chapel and halls, ornamented by Tudor brickwork. It too is surrounded by open green space that ignores the rage of traffic beyond the screening buildings. This is less gardenesque than the Fields, with stately stretches of mown green grass, embanked on one side and shaded by huge London plane trees that cast flickering shadows over the still greensward, and herbaceous borders. Be sure to visit the nearby cloisters.

GRAY'S INN
WC1

Gray's Inn is less pretty than Lincoln's Inn but even older and more resonant with history. In the early fourteenth century there was a manor here, owned by Sir Reginald le Gray, and this became a school of law. Those associated with the Inn include Henry VIII's bureaucrat Thomas Cromwell, Elizabeth I's trusty Lord Burleigh, the Carolean martyr Archbishop Laud, the historian and poet Lord Macaulay and statesman Lord Birkenhead, better known as F.E. Smith. Francis Bacon, a contemporary of Shakespeare, made a particular mark upon the place. He lived here for thirty years until his death in 1626 and his essays are marked 'from my chamber at Grais Inn'. He was much involved in the choice of planting and planning of 'the Walks', which became a special favourite of diarist Samuel Pepys, but have a darker association with duelling. The young Charles Dickens formed his first impressions of the perfidy of the law while he was working as a lawyer's clerk at Gray's Inn.

Gray's Inn suffered badly during the Blitz in the Second World War, and many of the buildings are either new or

Above The gardens of Gray's Inn offer a peaceful retreat during a summer lunchtime.

reconstructions of the originals. Thankfully, some features were stored away from London, so stained glass windows and a superb carved screen, reputedly made from the timbers of the ships of the Spanish Armada of 1588, were preserved. They have been replaced in the Hall, where Shakespeare's *Comedy of Errors* was first performed.

The long garden of Gray's Inn was once an ancient route from the rural area that is now north London to the City markets, a routeway commemorated in the central Great Walk still to be seen today. After a period of neglect, when rubbish mounted up and pits were formed by the removal of the gravel, the site was enclosed and kitchen gardens, pavilions, a mount and a bowling green were created. By the seventeenth century it had become a place where fashionable Londoners promenaded to see and be seen. Trees were planted in parallel rows and black ash or gravelled paths established formal walks between. Elms, limes and sycamores were the favoured trees but many succumbed to polluted air. There is a long upper terrace and a lower main routeway, with a grass bank between the two. Today this bank,

once a viewing point from which Highgate Hill could be seen, is ideal for sunbathing and the garden is a peaceful place for strolling, lunching on the grass or simply enjoying the green space beneath the wide canopies of London plane trees. A new oak tree avenue has been planted but it will be over a hundred years before this is truly established; we may hope that the continuity of this ancient garden is assured.

THE MIDDLE AND INNER TEMPLES
EC4

The name of London's Temple commemorates the Temple of Solomon in Jerusalem, and came to this spot with the crusading Order of the Knights Templar, who built a residence here in the twelfth century. When the Knights Templar were suppressed in 1312 their property came into the possession of the Knights Hospitallers, who leased part of it in about 1338 for use as a hostel for practitioners and students of the law. Though training was no doubt a strict and serious business, there are tales of some wild frolics – to the point of fox hunting *inside* the Middle Temple Hall. The Middle Temple also invited players from Bankside in seamy Southwark, across the river, to entertain them with a performance of Shakespeare's *Twelfth Night*. The Benchers, the governing bodies of the two Inns, remained tenants until 1609, when James I granted them ownership.

Among the great names associated with the Middle Temple shine those of Francis Drake and Walter Ralegh, William Wycherley and William Congreve, John Evelyn, Henry Fielding and Charles Dickens. Here Edmund Burke was consulted by the Founding Fathers on the drawing up of the Declaration of Independence and the American Constitution.

The Middle and Inner Temple gardens stretch down to the Embankment beside the river, and are among the oldest continuously used gardens in London. When the two Inns of the Temple became separate institutions, in 1732, the Inner Temple garden (the larger of the two) was divided into the Great Garden, the Nut Garden and Nuttery Court. The names of the two latter suggest that probably these fulfilled dual roles as orchards that were also ornamental; we know that later on plums, cherries and even nectarines were grown here.

Above, left to right Clematis tangutica, Arum creticum and Clematis 'Comtesse de Bouchaud' in the Inner Temple gardens.

Above Midday peace in the Fountain Court above the Middle Temple gardens.

Tradition has it that the adoption of red and white roses as symbols of the factions in the Wars of the Roses originated in the Middle Temple garden. The red rose (*Rosa gallica* var. *officinalis*) represented Lancaster and the white *Rosa × alba* 'Maxima' stood for York. Recently, in commemoration, sixteen plants of each have been planted in the border that runs along the Middle Temple gardens. With them, in token of peace, are sixteen plants of Rosa Mundi (*R. gallica* 'Versicolor'), a hybrid that has white petals splashed with crimson.

The main garden of the Inner Temple is still known as the Great Garden. Today it has a simple layout with spacious lawns and fine specimen trees. The Middle Temple garden has a raised area beside the Middle Temple Hall, with flowering and evergreen shrubs. It is mostly private but easily seen from the pretty Fountain Court, which still has a single spurt of water as it did in Charles Dickens' day. It was beside this fountain that Dickens had John Westlock meet Ruth Pinch in *Martin Chuzzlewit*. Note the very old wisteria that winds in the iron railings at the boundary between Fountain Court and the gardens.

In May 1888 the Royal Horticultural Society held a small garden show in the Inner Temple gardens. It was so successful that it continued to be held there every year until 1913, when, having outgrown the site, it was transferred to the Chelsea Royal Hospital (see page 97).

While visiting the gardens, look also for the superb brick King's Bench Walk on the eastern side, designed by Sir Christopher Wren. Another remarkable feature is the largely twelfth-century Temple Church, which has a Gothic nave leading to a circular Romanesque end which dates back to 1185. The transitional style of this period is still evident, despite intervention from – among others – Wren and Decimus Burton.

RUSSELL SQUARE

WC1

In the late eighteenth century, as the westward expansion of London accelerated, the 5th Duke of Bedford, like many of his fellow landowners, realized that money was to be made out of property. He pulled down the old family house and used Bedford land to develop the Bloomsbury estate between Euston Square and Holborn. The area, genteelly residential, provided elegant houses in Georgian terraces interspersed with squares.

Russell Square, laid out in 1800 for Lord William Russell, a Bedford, is the centrepiece of the whole scheme and the largest of the squares. It has gates at all four corners, served by serpentine paths that lead to a central horseshoe-shaped path around an open space. In the centre, shaded by tall plane trees, is a fountain plaza. The jets may be small, unassuming bubbling

springs or evolve into spectacular gushing jets, all thanks to twentieth-century computer control. When the water is switched off the plaza can be used as performance space.

Russell Square was one of Humphry Repton's few London schemes. It is formally planned, as if set beside a grand house rather than perceived as a landscape. Recently the square has been restored to resemble its former design; the iron railings and ornamental gates are interpretations of those removed during the Second World War, to support the war effort. As part of the restoration there is to be a lime tree cloister, a tunnel of clipped limes.

The planting is Regency in flavour, with inner and outer lawns separated by informal beds where shrubs and roses mix with herbaceous plants, which include some – such as cistus, phlomis and Spanish broom – imported from gentler climates. Dwarf mignonette, pinks and violets have replaced clipped box edging. Still a focal point is the tall statue of Francis, 5th Duke of Bedford; a member of the first Board of Agriculture, he has one hand on a plough and the other holds a stalk of corn.

BLOOMSBURY SQUARE

WC1

The Domesday Book records that part of Bloomsbury had vineyards and 'wood for 100 pigs'. In 1660 the Earl of Southampton built a house with an area beside it to the south that was to become Bloomsbury Square. Today Bloomsbury is the main university quarter of London, dominated by academic institutions, hospitals and the British Museum. Such august communities own many of the fine Georgian terraces of the area. Culture and the arts have always been Bloomsbury's lifeblood and it has been home to many literary intellectuals. Notably, in the twentieth century the members of the Bloomsbury Group – including Vanessa and Clive Bell, Virginia and Leonard Woolf, Duncan Grant, Lytton Strachey, E.M.

Forster, Bertrand Russell and John Maynard Keynes – gave to the area, and took from it, a lasting identity.

The elegant terraces of Bloomsbury Square were laid out in the early 1800s, replacing houses of the 1660s. The designer was James Burton, father of Decimus, and as soon as the terraces were completed the square became the height of fashion. Famous residents include essayist Sir Richard Steele, collector Sir Hans Sloane and, later, architect Sir Edwin Lutyens.

The square was once gravelled but in the eighteenth century funds were provided for planting and maintenance. Humphry Repton influenced the layout and it is thought that he introduced some flower beds. Sadly, though, today the garden no longer exists. Sir Richard Westmacott's 1816 statue of the political and rakish Charles James Fox is still there and London plane trees provide shade.

Above Looking south across the newly restored garden of Russell Square.

FITZROY SQUARE

W1

Architecturally this is one of the finest squares in London. It was built by the 1st Baron Southampton, Augustus Henry Fitzroy, a great-great-grandson of Charles II. In the early 1790s terraced houses, designed by the Adam brothers, were built on the east and south sides. After 1825 further elegant terraces on the west and north sides completed the enclosure. The south side was destroyed by bombing in the Second World War.

In 1815 the residents, finding fault with the central space which they described as a 'cow yard' and 'the playground of children of the lowest classes', set about turning it into a private place of trees and shrubs for residents. The square's garden as we see it today is a subtle twentieth-century design by Sir Geoffrey Jellicoe. Set in pedestrian-only surroundings, the circular garden is railing-ringed with only one gate, ensuring

Above Fine terraces surrounding Fitzroy Square are partially concealed by huge old plane trees that add to the seclusion of the grassy square.

seclusion. The centre is an open undulating green-turfed garden, with plane trees giving some shade around the perimeter. Only one feature distracts the eye, a fibreglass sculpture made by Naomi Blake in 1977 to commemorate the Queen's Silver Jubilee, set on a diagonal plinth which to my mind is at odds with the garden's curvaceous informality.

The square has distinguished associations with the arts. The Pre-Raphaelite Brotherhood met regularly at No. 37, which was the home of the American writer Ford Madox Brown; writers George Bernard Shaw and Virginia Woolf both lived at No. 29 and Roger Fry set up the Omega workshops at No. 33.

BRITISH LIBRARY
WC1

The new British Library has a spectacular piazza, dominated by a powerfully fine piece, Eduardo Paolozzi's bronze of Isaac Newton. Below this is a large circular horizontally planed garden-sculpture, designed by Anthony Gormley. The piazza is wisely low key, a contemplative space ringed with concentrically clipped box hedges – reminiscent of classical amphitheatres, which need people to animate their stone simplicity. Large rough glacial boulders are carefully set at regular intervals on immaculate plinths around the arena. These fragments of 'meteors', which seem to have been collected and carved with primitive simplicity, show the human form clinging and burrowing into the security of rock – a contrast to the certitude of the Paolozzi sculpture.

CALTHORPE PROJECT COMMUNITY GARDEN
WC1

Alongside Gray's Inn Road is an unexpected area of 1½ acres of greenery that has been saved from office development by the local community. The energy and commitment of those who give their time or work here is impressive. Many are volunteers, including people with learning difficulties, and they support the regular staff. Over twenty years they have succeeded in creating a lovely and exciting community garden. The short lease is regularly and generously extended by Camden Borough Council, which has set the social value of the site higher than its commercial value.

Environmental concerns are a priority in the garden. The main timber building is of particular interest. It is a Walter Segal self-build kit made of environmentally treated timber that bolts together and stands on stilts. There is a compact wildlife area that is very successful and the garden has many songbirds. A workshop area has greenhouses for teaching willow-weaving and other rural crafts, as well as classes in horticulture, held in association with Kingsway College, on subjects such as how to grow from seeds. Teaching gardening using organic methods is an important function of the site.

Sports pitches are a great draw, as is a children's playground. One paved area is used for organized events such as Peruvian panpipe or salsa bands. There is art too, made on site, including mosaic pictures on the entrance path and a superb wall painting along the high brick-walled boundary of the pitches.

Above all this is a tranquil garden, an escape from the inner city. It is divided into intimate areas. Seclusion can be found inside a circular enclosure hedged with hornbeam. Some more open grassed spaces are ideal for family picnics. One area is imaginatively secret with decorated benches around a tiny stream and pond, all hidden beneath a bridged entrance. Here yellow *Rosa xanthina* 'Canary Bird' starts the summer, with lilacs and other flowering shrubs, and set into this space is a weeping grey-leaved silver pear (*Pyrus salicifolia* 'Pendula') with clematis growing on it. Elsewhere flowering cherries and crab apples provide canopies of shade over the undulating grassy landscape and a ginkgo creates a strong focus.

The garden is popular and much loved, and many visitors come from abroad to study the community-based project with the aim of setting up something similar in their own cities.

NEW RIVER WALK

N1

The New River is surprisingly old, being the 40 mile fresh-water canal completed in 1613 by Sir Hugh Myddelton to carry drinkable spring water into central London, following the 100 feet/30 metre contour line (see page 61). The part that runs through Islington is one of the surviving channels with wooden revetments – restored in 1954 – and offers a slim lengthy walk, mostly fringed with trees, shrubs and summer flowers.

Alongside Canonbury Grove the path meanders past large water-worn limestone rocks which form tiny waterfalls and pools scaled down for children and popular as paddling pools for ducks. The plants along the walk are a mixture of wild and ornamental – self-sown valerian, teasels and flag irises mix pleasingly with yellow columns of lysimachia and hostas, while weeping willows and shrub elders merge with specimen trees that include sweet gum (*Liquidambar styraciflua*) and ornamental viburnums. There is a charming late-eighteenth-century round house, built for the linesman who looked after the waterway and ensured that the water stayed clean – no bathing or fishing were allowed.

MALVERN TERRACE

N1

Front gardens are a characteristic of old London because roads were unpleasantly muddy and separation from the house was felt essential. Nowadays such front gardens are often lost

Left The pretty mosaic path at the entrance to the Calthorpe Project invites everybody in.

beneath shop fronts. But some remain and are a source of pleasure for both owner and passer-by.

In Barnsbury there is a row of pretty early Victorian cottages in a cobbled cul-de-sac. These have beautifully kept long front gardens, each planned in quite different styles. Some are formal, with direct access to the front door and planted structurally using fastigiate yews and clippable evergreens. Others have an informal flavour in which the garden area is treated as one unit, so no specific path is defined. There are wisteria-clad walls and roses in profusion, sometimes almost hiding the door. Summer flowers include campanulas, geraniums, sisyrinchiums and asters, growing with roses, hydrangeas and elegant Japanese maples. Overhead small ornamental trees flower in summer and are coppered in autumn. The gardens can be visited under the Yellow Book scheme.

CULPEPER COMMUNITY GARDENS
N1

Land is at a premium in the borough of Islington. The closely packed terraced housing has courtyards rather than gardens and local authority apartment blocks have only balconies.

The inspiration to offer people without their own gardens the chance to become true gardeners came from a temporary community garden made in the 1970s by people living around Covent Garden. In Islington the White Lion Free School, in co-operation with Penton Primary School, took over a derelict area in 1980. The notion of a garden for children was widened to include the whole community; and with luck it was found that the borough had allocated this area to become public space, so money for the project was forthcoming. A team was set up to draft a constitution: one founding member, Roz Dunwell, was a full-time paid employee, and she was backed

Right Canonbury Grove gives access to the revitalized New River Walk.

by a team of volunteers. The garden was properly designed and laid out with cleaned soil and children were involved with planning.

To find the garden, go though a hole in the wall by the King of Denmark pub in Cloudesley Road. The gloriously filled open space is awash with healthy flowers and overflowing foliage. Many individual passions create a carnival of mixed summer colour. Parts of the garden are communally run, while in others people have been given plots to do their own thing. Some were already frustrated gardeners, others beginners. Many cultures are represented in the choice of plants, which include a variety of exotic vegetables; and annuals consort with perennials and vegetables with herbs in the same easy manner as the different members of the community here work side by side.

Even when summer is at its most effulgent, the underlying garden plan, designed on clean lines, is never quite obscured. Arbours and pergolas give structure to the communally run sections and provide shade beneath rambles of pink and white roses, wisteria, clematis and honeysuckle. There is a wildlife area with a small pool where water bugs are studied, and a larger pool invites more of nature to settle, among flag irises and lysimachia. In addition there is the essential English stretch of mown grass, there for those who simply enjoy lying on it or padding about with bare feet on a hot day. A large specimen weeping ash *Fraxinus excelsior* 'Pendula' grows well in the grass and another weeper, the silver pear (*Pyrus salicifolia* 'Pendula'), adds style.

Anyone who has no garden of their own is welcome to take an active part here. The garden is all about sharing and caring, and self-seeding plants like pink and red valerian and creamy sisyrinchium are allowed the same freedom as people, distributing themselves everywhere, and by serendipity the garden links together in contented unity. Although the garden is superbly organized, in fact the few do not simply run it for the many; the many are involved throughout.

Above In Islington, where there is a dearth of parks, flowery front gardens like those of Malvern Terrace have a special value.
Right The precious space of Culpeper Gardens is crammed with flowers, fruit, vegetables and trees, all cared for by the local community.

CAMLEY STREET NATURAL PARK
NW1

Around King's Cross railway terminus, where the Regent's Canal cuts through a grim maze of polluted industrial concrete, there is an internationally acclaimed 'wilderness' park for the community. In the 1980s the site was derelict, destined by the Greater London Council to become a coach and lorry park. But with vision and tenacity local people lobbied the authority until funds were found for a project-officer-cum-park-manager to run it as a nature reserve, and a teaching post was funded by the Inner London Education Authority.

Work began in 1983, much of the labour being shared with volunteers. Illegal waste dumping was the first problem, followed by the need to restore soil conditions, dig out large connecting ponds and establish an ecological balance. The park was formally opened in May 1985. Its aims are to conserve nature and offer recreation. The scheme has been so successful that the co-operative partnership now has more staff, acting as community involvement officers; and the area has become a wonderful place for people and wildlife, with a visitors' centre to unite the two.

The long quiet water, lush green meadow and dappled woodland create varying habitats for a rich diversity of animal and plant life. Frogs, toads, newts and water snails are secreted within thick flag iris, rush, marsh marigold, bogbean and pond sedge. Skating water boatmen, hovering damselflies and flashes of dragonflies appear in summer. The meadow is filled with native plants including cow parsley, foxtail, cranesbill and campion, protecting many beetles, bees and butterflies. Shrubs such as elder, guelder rose, spindles, blackthorn, dog roses and self-sown buddlejas provide thick cover for birds as well as

Left Camley Street Natural Park could be in the country, but for the skeletal frames of old gasometers seen through the trees.
Opposite Just as unexpected in a concreted industrial area is the Cross Club's small exotic garden, where all the plants thrive in containers.

insects. Hawthorn, rowan, field maple, wild cherry, alder, aspen and shrub willows are everywhere, masking the skeletal frames of gasholders and spires of St Pancras station. It is easy to forget that this is inner London.

School groups visit regularly in term time to follow seasonal nature trails set by the spring colours of cowslips, primroses and bluebells, and the summer meadows with poppies, ox-eye daisies and even the occasional common spotted orchid, a treasured interloper. In autumn seed heads, colourful, fluffy and explosive, provoke interest. Throughout the long school holiday there is an environmental summer scheme. In autumn there is apple day in October and tree dressing day in December. Every May the annual festival, with music as a highlight, welcomes people from all parts of London. Such an invitation is characteristic of the park: it is for people and all are welcome. A walk along the meandering pond-side path, a visit to the quiet canal where long boats tie up or a picnic beside the visitors' centre – any of these makes a restorative excursion for city dwellers.

CROSS CLUB

NW1

Underneath railway arches near King's Cross station is a deeply set nightclub which has several outdoor areas that bring the character of the Mediterranean, the South Seas and Asia to a once industrial site. Large specimen plants in containers, including bamboo, feather palms, cordylines, olive trees, Italian cypress and umbrella pines show a relaxed attitude to mixing plants. Atmosphere is what counts and both Shiva and Buddha set the eclectic style. The floors are either timber-decked or designed with recycled paving, such as old cobblestones from warehouses, marble pieces set into concrete and solid timber railway sleepers. There is a timber and thatched garden bar with a flavour of the Pacific Islands and overhead white 'sails' stretched to catch every breeze as if on a sailing ship.

ROYAL FORESTS AND WILDERNESS

COCKFOSTERS, ENFIELD AND EPPING

ROYAL FORESTS AND WILDERNESS
Cockfosters, Enfield and Epping

Myddelton House, Forty Hall, Hilly Fields, Grovelands Park, Capel Manor, Lee Valley Regional Park, Epping Forest, Wanstead Park, Hainault Forest

In north and east outer London there are some lovely, relatively untouched green areas where kings once hunted. One such is the borough of Enfield, formerly part of the vast royal forest of Enfield Chase. In 1777 an Act was passed declaring that 'the Chase in its present State yields very little profit' either to the Crown or the freeholders and the land was divided between the Crown and the bordering parishes. Some areas of the forest were enclosed but some were retained as common land, while others became the fine parks that abound in the Enfield area.

Poverty as well as profit denuded much of the remaining parts of the ancient forest, with the stripping of trees for firewood destroying many of them. In 1815 the Royal Small Arms Factory was built at Waltham Abbey, offering employment and thereby saving the region. As the railways and Underground made commuting possible, and London spread outwards, small villages within the forest were merged into the urban mass. Further losses of land occurred in the suburbanization of the 1930s, when many orchards and nurseries were covered over by mass housing.

Some of the mansions of the area have gone, but their estates are now open to the public. Examples include Forty Hall, built in 1629–36; the parkland around Grovelands, built in 1797; and Hilly Fields, once grazing land.

The borough of Enfield is also home to a horticultural college, Capel Manor Gardens, and, to the east, making a natural boundary, the Lee Valley Regional Park. This is a managed area of marshes and meadows around the River Lee, which penetrates London to the River Thames. Unlike many of London's rivers, it has not been covered over. Today there is a fine walk from the East End, following the River Lee Navigation Route, through the park, to Ware, Hertfordshire. Early market gardens and nurseries of Hackney overspilled along the Lea Valley, through Tottenham, Edmonton and Enfield, and even now some of the family associations with nurserymen, seedsmen, market gardeners and florists continue in the area,

Beyond the River Lee is the great Epping Forest, an ancient forest also once favoured for hunting by kings and their courtiers, and a remarkable survival. Despite many incursions by roads and developers, it is still a wonderfully rural place with over 6,000 acres of indigenous planting.

Epping Forest extends southwards to include Wanstead Flats, and on to Wanstead Park, a former private estate with the remains of dramatic watery landscaping. To the east of the area, where the ancient forest of Essex survives as Hainault Forest, is more saved coutryside. Here are semi-wooded slopes offering wonderful views over the City and the river.

MYDDELTON HOUSE
ENFIELD, MIDDLESEX

This house, built by the Bowles family in 1814, is named for Sir Hugh Myddelton, the rich, imaginative entrepreneur who undertook the building of the New River from Chadwell and Amwell in Hertfordshire (see page 50).

In the first half of the twentieth century E.A. Bowles was in possession of the house and garden. A passionate plantsman and botanical artist, he made the 4-acre garden a place for his plant collection, the fruits of his own and others' travels. It included some unlikely rarities: plants with unusual habit, planted in an area of the garden which he referred to as 'the lunatic asylum', a collection of cacti and another of plants with coloured leaves, known as 'Tom Tiddler's ground'.

Though Bowles' collection no longer exists, surviving from his time is a rock garden in poor shape and a large well-maintained lake with water plants and carp. Originally fresh water for the lake was drawn from a branch of the New River that swerved along the southern boundary. This was filled in about fifty years ago and replaced by a charming grassed terrace walk which ends under the old iron footbridge where the river once flowed, unfortunately now stopping abruptly with a bed of cacti that seems almost stuffed under the bridge. The grassed walk is bordered by beds where tulips and irises are displayed, this being the home of the national iris collection.

The garden is renowned for spreading carpets of naturalized spring bulbs; there are over a hundred different snowdrops and crocus species. In autumn, cyclamen, zephyranthes, nerines,

crinums and colchicums appear. Trees include the foxglove tree (*Paulownia tomentosa*), a fine specimen of the twisted Harry Lauder's walking stick (*Corylus avellana* 'Contorta') and the shrub Carolina allspice (*Calycanthus floridus*).

The garden is pleasing, with many interesting and intimate corners and a meadow walk that is wonderful in spring and summer. Now owned by the Lee Valley Water Authority, the garden is gradually being restored, no easy task as Bowles' plant knowledge was highly specialized.

FORTY HALL
ENFIELD, MIDDLESEX

Close to Myddelton House is Forty Hall, also with connections to the Bowles family, who bought it at the end of the nineteenth century. This superb family house of elegantly judged proportions was built in 1629 for a Lord Mayor of London, Sir Nicholas Rainton. The grounds are pleasant, with a lake, roses, a magnificent very old cedar, woodland and a pretty meadow walk down to the Turkey Brook. Where the road crosses the brook is the site of an old Roman bridge. It is also rumoured to be the place where Elizabeth I was invited to step upon Sir Walter Ralegh's cloak to avoid the mud, but, as with the whereabouts of King Arthur's round table, many other places lay claim to the story. Sadly for Enfield, Greenwich Park is a more likely location.

There is a charming walled garden with a collection of shrub roses in island beds that make 'wings' for summer productions of Shakespeare plays. In the front are groups of winter-flowering fragrant witch hazels, followed in spring by scented azaleas.

HILLY FIELDS
ENFIELD, MIDDLESEX

One of the most charming public spaces in the Enfield area, Hilly Fields was old grazing land, once part of Enfield Chase, that was snapped up by Enfield Urban District Council in 1911

Pages 56–57 Huge old beech trees in Epping Forest, pollarded long ago, reflect low winter sunlight on their smooth silver bark.
Page 58 An ancient cedar of Lebanon, probably planted in the late seventeenth century, frames the Jacobean mansion of Forty Hall.
Left The glory lily (*Gloriosa superba* 'Rothschildiana') from tropical Africa and India, growing in the conservatory at Myddelton House.

to make a country park of 62 acres. This wonderful site is open to surrounding roads because the municipal railings were melted down during the Second World War, as part of the war effort. Best approached from Phipps Hatch Lane, the parkland is hilly, with oak trees at the crest of the hill and fine old Scots pines along one side. Grass sweeps down to the Turkey Brook, where the stream meanders peacefully and children and dogs have a great time.

Part of the site has now become a Site of Special Scientific Interest because of a rare species of ant that thrives in the open meadowland. Fortunately Hilly Fields is set within the conservation area of the Green Belt, and the Friends of Hilly Fields, using a grant from the Heritage Lottery Fund, guard it well and have recently restored the old bandstand.

Above Light penetrates through the trees on the upper level of Hilly Fields.

GROVELANDS PARK
N14

Around the private hospital that is now Grovelands Priory there is a late-eighteenth-century landscape park and lake. John Nash built the house in 1797 for Walker Gray, who had connections with the famous Walker cricketing family, owners of the nearby Arnos estate.

The grounds were designed by Humphry Repton. They slope gently down to a shallow valley and include a lake, made by damming the Bourne stream, with two islands where waterfowl live undisturbed. The surrounding oak woodland, although much reduced in the 1930s to build houses, is still very pleasant, with undulating terrain and a tumbling brook that winds around large boulders, placed to look like outcrops but quite unnatural for the area, so surely part of the romantic Repton scheme. The local authority purchased the park early in the twentieth century and soon afterwards Thomas H. Mawson was employed as its landscape architect.

There is a polygonal walled kitchen garden that is no longer in use but which has hot walls. Here peaches, nectarines, vines and other exotic delicacies were grown in the lean-to greenhouses. A partly sunken brick-built glasshouse remains from the eighteenth century. This part of the garden and the lawns around the house are private, but the house can be seen from the open grounds around the lake, now a public park, despite being physically sealed off by a ha-ha. However, as the local authority has allowed some of the trees and shrubs to spread, it is now not so easy to see the view of the house across the lake as Repton intended.

Recently, necessary but rather municipal-looking restoration work reinforcing the dam and outflow has been carried out

Right The Bourne stream winds through old oak woodland around the carefully placed landscape of rocks in Grovelands Park.

and the associated planting is functional, combining ornamental shrubs with willows. This spreading shrubbery lacks charm and makes it difficult to see the waterfowl from the path. A programme of careful thinning is needed.

The walk through the woods is much enjoyed in winter and summer by families and dogs. There are sports facilities too, including a good 'pitch and putt' green near the Inverforth Gates, off the Bourne, and a fenced-off, very popular playground.

CAPEL MANOR
ENFIELD, MIDDLESEX

An attractive Georgian house, Capel Manor is today home to a successful horticultural college. The old stable block has been converted and there are new outbuildings and lecture theatres, as well as a fine library. Surrounding the manor are the original gardens with large established trees including a copper beech, a tulip tree, Scots pines and a huge zelkova. The red bricks of the walled garden date from the late eighteenth century, with a further 4 feet/1.2 metres added in Victorian times. There is a pool with a small waterfall, edged with Japanese acers and waterside plants. Around the perimeter of the old garden are many different species of holly, and a modern maze, also made of holly, has been planted.

The primary role of the garden today is that of a teaching garden. The college provides training at all levels, with courses on horticulture, groundsmanship, arboriculture, ecology, design, floristry and many allied themes, with full- and part-time programmes that lead to professional qualifications. There is much to see. A map from the visitor centre is essential and may be studied over refreshments in a pleasant restaurant.

Left Different hedging possibilities are demonstrated in Capel Manor gardens. Each hedge, formal or informal, ends with its 'parent', untouched by pruning, showing how some hedging plants are potentially very tall trees.

Some visitors come specially to see the small sponsored demonstration gardens of different designs, exploring materials and plants. Not all are successful but some, like the Japanese Garden, are very interesting.,

For me the most agreeable area is that of the large water lily lake, which is thickly planted with reeds, willows and other bog plants. Here the visitor can stroll or rest in the shade of twisted willows (*Salix contorta*), watching the fleeting animation of insects and birds crossing the surface and the flash of golden orfe beneath. A coolly white Arcadian arbour sets the scene with classic simplicity. Near by a rustic summerhouse built of recycled bricks and timbers creates quite a different mood.

But the most fascinating area is the trial grounds, sponsored by *Which?* garden magazine. The large space is divided by two superb sets of very tall hedges with high, wide arches. One area has rows of different types of clipped hedging, including berberis, laurel, conifer, privet, beech, olearia, forsythia and, the most informal, *Rosa rugosa*. At the end of each hedge is one unclipped specimen, revealing that some hedging plants, such as leylandii or hornbeam, are really forest-sized trees. A group of 'synchronized gardens' compares pruning methods. The same plants, given the same conditions, are pruned, semi-trimmed, held back, dead-headed or simply left alone. The national collection of achilleas is here, so colours, sizes and foliage can be compared. Beds given over to crocosmias show differences in flower power and habit. Trials of new cultivars and beds for annuals catch the eye. And the Low-allergen Garden, with no wind-pollinated plants, tells a tale. The trials include practicalities like fencing methods.

Rare breeds of animals are on show, including pigs and Clydesdale horses. In the summer there are specialist weekends, festivals, special garden events, horse shows, vintage car displays and musical evenings, all ensuring the value of the garden to the community.

LEE VALLEY REGIONAL PARK

For centuries the River Lee, or Lea (it is spelt both ways), was essential for transporting goods from the River Thames to the outer reaches of London – in its day a sort of watery M1. The river's value, for supplying mills and fisheries, was recognized in 1424 by legislation and about two hundred years later the first inland waterway lock was built at Waltham Abbey. Eighteenth-century navigation channels improved matters further.

Today it provides a treasured green thread of open space. In recent years the twenty-six miles from the East India Dock on the River Thames to Ware in Hertfordshire have been managed so that there are countryside areas, urban green spaces, parks, nature reserves, lakes and riverside trails. A leaflet with a map, obtainable from the information centre at Waltham Abbey, shows the many points of access to the park.

In 1993, a route following the course of the river was opened – a green walk of fifty miles. Starting near Canary Wharf towers, the River Lee Navigation Route through the park follows the semi-tidal river Bow, along towpaths, through tunnels and under bridges, all restored. Narrow boats are moored along the towpaths and there is a canoe centre at the Lee Valley Marina. The river passes a leisure complex at Pickett's Lock and the old Gunpowder Mills at Waltham Abbey.

Sometimes running parallel with the Navigation Route and sometimes diverging along the main river and its tributaries, footpaths lead into open spaces of replanned parkland and new nature reserves, where once industrial buildings stood and the marshland was impassable. With newly planted trees, the riverside walks offer some of the pleasantest 'green lungs' of the capital, enjoyed by cyclists, riders, anglers, campers and birdwatchers as well as walkers. For those committed to nature conservation there are marshes with wetland habitats and meadows, some of which are Sites of Special Scientific Interest. At Walthamstow Marshes ecologists have found 340 plant species and claim some hybrids to be unique to the area.

Diversions may be made to places of historical interest, including the Huguenot House Mill at Three Mills Island, near Bromley-by-Bow, and the water works at Lammas Road, both landscaped and becoming major cultural centres. At Enfield Lock, Enfield Island Village is being built on the site of the Royal Small Arms Factory, famous for the Lee-Enfield rifle. Parts of the old industrial buildings have been recycled as homes or community use. A row of new houses beside the river at Turpin Close has deservedly won the Enfield in Bloom competition for two years running. By the lock rows of old cottages backing on to the river and fronting the canal have been restored.

Above Restored Victorian cottages beside Enfield Lock, which is part of the long Lee Valley walk.

EPPING FOREST

EPPING, ESSEX

Epping Forest is one of London's greatest treasures: a place of wonderful variety, with undulating land, open glades, grazing meadows, dense woodland and sunken marshes, and over 150 ponds. Roads and a profusion of footpaths cross it and yet there are many places of quiet stillness.

Woodland, grassland, heath and marsh mean diverse plants and habitats. Over three hundred species of wild flowers grow here. There are indicators of site conditions, such as adder's tongue, a small rare fern of ancient grassland; heather, indicating acidic heaths; gorse in acidic sandy soil; and cotton grass and sundew, which revel in areas of permanently damp soil. Beech and birch dominate the lighter soils, oak and hornbeam the heavier; this is the largest forest of hornbeam trees in England. The age of the forest is indicated by field maple (*Acer campestre*), butcher's broom (*Ruscus aculeatus*) and wild service trees (*Sorbus torminalis*), all of which are characteristic of ancient woodlands. The Nature Conservancy Council has designated the forest as a Site of Special Scientific Interest for the many birds, butterflies and, famously, over 1,200 species of beetle that inhabit it.

With the city so close, all this needs sensitive management, which is achieved by a combination of ancient rights and modern authorities. There is a source of information about the forest at the Epping Forest Conservation Centre at High Beech, which is managed by the Field Studies Council. Here an environmental education service exists for children of all ages and also offers guided walks. The Corporation of London own the forest and continue to protect its character in partnership with local people, English Nature, English Heritage, the Forestry Commission and the Countryside Agency.

Epping Forest is a remnant of ancient wooded land that throve after the last Ice Age from the Wash to the Thames, long before the Romans established Londinium. There are indications of early Mesolithic settlement, roughly 10,000 years old, near High Beech, and Iron Age earthworks have been found at Ambresbury Banks and Loughton Camp. Romantic but unproven associations with Boudicca, Queen of the Iceni tribe who fought the Romans, have been suggested.

In 1030 Waltham Abbey was founded near by and King Harold, he of the Bayeux Tapestry who was killed at Hastings in 1066, is thought to be buried there. When, after his death, the Normans took over the country, hunting became the sport of kings and both Henry VIII and his daughter Elizabeth I followed the hunt in the forest. The forest proved a rich source of 'black' deer, which still live here today in a special sanctuary, and the Abbey provided lodging for hunting royals. Elizabeth used a hunting lodge at Chingford as a grandstand to watch the chase. This now houses Epping Forest Museum.

In 1226 the right was granted to citizens of London to hunt on Easter Monday and the Easter Hunt became an annual celebration. From the Middle Ages, the forest was used as well for grazing land and timber. Systematic pollarding has resulted in the deformed habits of some older trees.

By the seventeenth century the forest ceased to draw royal attention, so strict controls were virtually abandoned. Enclosures reduced the area to 6,000 acres by 1851 and threatened to take more. In the 1860s Thomas Willingdale, an old labourer, shocked by yet more proposals to sell off the forest for building plots, reasserted the commoners' ancient lopping rights by way of the annual ceremony of lighting a fire on Staples Hill at midnight on 11 November. Partly as a result of this, the Commons Preservation Society was formed and, with the Corporation of London, effectively took the Lord of the Manor to court and put a stop to any further notion of building plots. Ultimately an Act of Parliament in 1878 ensured the forest's future, as the land was handed over to the Corporation of London and dedicated to the

people in perpetuity. Commoners kept their rights to collect firewood, and branches could be taken from certain trees. By this time, the Easter Hunt had degenerated into a bawdy drunken rout, and the last one took place in 1882.

Epping Forest is much loved and people go there to walk, ride, picnic and forget the city. For the more energetic, areas are set aside for cycling, football, golf, boating and swimming – even parascending is practised in Wanstead Flats.

It is light that makes woodland so magical. In summer one can have the quiet pleasure of walking in the dark cool shade beneath the canopy, which contrasts with surrounding heated urban streets. And in autumn sunlight intensifies the rust-coloured blankets of leaves that coat the undulating landscape. Winter can be miserable, but there are treasured days when shafts of misty bluish light focus through the powerful tree forms with theatrical effect.

WANSTEAD PARK

E11

Despite being encircled by suburbia, this stretch of parkland is as attractive as any in London. Walks follow the sinuously flowing course of a chain of lakes, which are remnants of an underlying, largely eighteenth-century, formal landscape and were built by diverting the River Roding. There are islands for large trees and waterfowl; wild water lilies skim the surface and reeds crowd the banks, giving cover to heron, moorhen and coot. In the woodland oak and sycamore dominate groups of birch, beech and willows that sometimes come right to the edge of the water. Restoration is in progress, so the newly concreted revetments that edge the water are exposed at present but will soon be covered again.

Left Dappled light beneath the trees in the undulating woodland of Epping Forest.

Above A family walk in spacious Wanstead Park, where traces of an eighteenth-century landscape are evident.

The park has a complicated history of ownership. There was a Roman villa here and there are associations with Mary Tudor and Elizabeth I, but the land was not enclosed until the sixteenth century. Wanstead House was built with ambitious pretension in 1715; its position is now occupied by a golf course. The landscaping was commissioned then. Inheritance passed the property on to Catherine Wellesley Pole, who cleared her debts by selling off the contents and demolishing the house in 1824.

The site has an air of the wild, with rough grassland, dense thickets of holly or hawthorn, and undergrowth of gorse and rhododendrons. But reminders of past glory appear unexpectedly – as with the façade of an old grotto on the shore of the Ornamental Water, which is all that remains of the mansion. This is a shadow of its former self, when it was roofed and studded with shells, pebbles, crystals, mirrors, stalactites and coloured glass windows. The classically inspired Temple is

more visible, being the focus for an avenue of young sweet chestnut trees that will one day be magnificent. At present, these are subtly footed with native dog roses in delicate shades of pale pink. The whole site is carefully managed by the Corporation of London, which bought it in 1882 and added it to Epping Forest. Natural regeneration is the Corporation's policy, although care is taken to retain the 'bones' of the former landscaping.

Near by is the fine Georgian church of St Mary the Virgin, consecrated in 1790 and designed by Thomas Hardwick, a peaceful place, set in a romantically overgrown graveyard amidst the dark shade cast by fine old trees including bay, yew and massive horse chestnuts. Otherwise the site is open. Swathes of uncut grass and moss conceal flat gravestones, such as that of the Astronomer Royal, the Reverend James Bradley, a resident of Wanstead House and a contemporary of Isaac

Newton. Lumpish mounds of ivy completely conceal upright graves, and occasional roses give splashes of vibrant colour where they have survived the onslaught of nature.

HAINAULT FOREST
HAINAULT, ESSEX

Like Epping Forest, Hainault Forest, originally part of the estates of the abbey of Barking, is a fragment of the ancient Royal Forest of Essex. The hilly land, providing dense thickets of trees and shrubs with cleared meadows in between, made it perfect hunting ground. The forest was managed to supply timber for building and fuel. Some old pollarded hornbeams can still be seen and some of the ancient oaks and beech survive today. The last monarch to hunt here was Charles II; after his reign the hunting deteriorated as deer poaching became common.

By the mid-Victorian era, large areas of the forest had been felled for agriculture. The efforts of Mr E. Buxton, an Epping forester, alerted public authorities to the potential loss and in 1903 the 900 acres of mixed woodland, plantations, heath, marsh, meadow, farmland and lakes were purchased by the London County Council for public use in perpetuity. Trees were replanted, and groves of holly and hawthorn re-established themselves. Today glades and meadows are managed for wild flowers – the area is rich in flora and fauna, making it a wonderful place for a 'day in the country'. From the hill there is a commanding prospect of the City of London.

Left and right Hainault Forest has open stretches of meadow as well as secluded woodland walks.

UP WEST –
CHURCH
AND STATE

THE WEST END,
ST JAMES'S AND
WESTMINSTER

UP WEST – CHURCH AND STATE
The West End, St James's and Westminster

Berkeley Square, Grosvenor Square, Mount Street Gardens, St James's Park, Green Park, Victoria Embankment Gardens, Victoria Tower Gardens, Westminster Abbey, Chester Square, Eccleston Square

Before George IV decided to build Buckingham Palace, which Queen Victoria was to make the main official home for the royal family as it is today, St James's Palace, built by Henry VIII, was the principal residence of the royals. Henry enclosed nearby land for hunting, and this was developed by subsequent monarchs to become St James's Park and Green Park, the first of the royal parks. Situated close to Buckingham Palace, these parks maintain their royal connections today, and provide green open spaces in the heart of the capital that are enjoyed by tourists and Londoners alike.

Being convenient for the Court of St James, close to the great parks and removed from densely populated areas, Mayfair became part of London's continued expansion west in the eighteenth century. The name commemorates fairs held here in May from the late seventeenth to the mid-eighteenth centuries. In this part of London between Oxford Street, Piccadilly, Regent's Street and Park Lane aristocratic Londoners built mansions, wide straight roads and large formal squares such as Berkeley and Grosvenor Squares, named after the landholding families. The area became the most fashionable in London, and the open, formally paved squares places to be seen. In the early eighteenth century, Thomas Fairchild, writing in *The City Gardener*, promoted the idea of squares being gardened to represent a rural idyll, with 'groves and wildernesses', 'shady and private' walks, a 'Harbour for Birds', so that 'every Quarter would hide the Prospect of the Houses', all themes familiar to today's gardeners. But in Mayfair only in the central pleasance of Grosvenor Square was this idea really carried out.

Mayfair is no longer a truly residential area, having been taken over by embassies and clubs, banks and advertisers, car showrooms and airlines. The large squares, many of them managed by the Grosvenor estate, have become rather municipal in character. The smaller squares, on the other hand, are often private and communally managed and sometimes gardened by residents, and there is much pleasing variety; many are open to the public on London Squares Day in June. Mount Street Gardens is a delightful public park, a retreat for anyone who works near by.

Besides the monarchy, the area includes the seats of other powers, Church and Parliament, near the river at Westminster. Each has associated gardens available to the public. The very old cloister gardens of Westminster Abbey, dating from the thirteenth century and later, are quiet and enclosed, so different from the public spaces around the Houses of Parliament, where showpieces are dominated by the brilliant bedding plants that celebrate summer.

BERKELEY SQUARE

W1

This square commemorates Lord Berkeley, the Royalist commander in the Civil War who owned much land, of which the square is but a remnant. Surrounded by long rows of houses, it was laid out to grass in the 1730s and remodelled in the early 1800s to include shrubberies. Today it is remarkable not for singing nightingales but for the thirty huge and handsome London plane trees, planted in 1789, and among the oldest and finest plane trees in London.

Still surviving on the west side are some superb mid-eighteenth century houses. Sir Nikolaus Pevsner described No. 44, built by William Kent in 1742 and now owned by the Claremont Club, as 'the finest terrace house of London'. The Prince Regent was a frequent visitor to No. 44 and entertainment can still be found there at Annabel's nightclub.

Distinguished figures who have been associated with the square include William Pitt the Elder and Charles James Fox.

GROSVENOR SQUARE
W1

This large square, built in the early eighteenth century and still owned by the Grosvenor estate, has always been upmarket, a place where the wealthy had beautiful houses. Influenced by Thomas Fairchild, the square was originally planted in 'the rural manner' as a wilderness, contained by hedging within an oval design, with wide turf walks among dwarf trees and low shrubs so that promenaders could see the fine surrounding architecture. The houses were designed by a distinguished list of architects, but only two remain from those gracious times.

The famous people who have lived here are legion. In the Second World War, many houses were taken for the US military, earning it the nickname 'Eisenhower Platz'. On the west side there is the enormous wide building of the United States Embassy. The American influence is reinforced by the central statue of President Franklin D. Roosevelt.

Pages 72–73 Relaxing in Green Park.
Page 75 One might expect to find red telephone boxes in Berkeley Square, but a gilded cow? This was a temporary summer adornment, part of a scheme sponsored by the Arts Council.
Left An ancient, knobbly London plane tree, one of thirty that were planted in Berkeley Square in 1789.
Right Gilding again, but this time on the American eagle, flying high over the United States Embassy in Grosvenor Square.

MOUNT STREET GARDENS
W1

Opened as a public park in 1880–90, Mount Street Gardens is on the site of old burial ground that served the local churches until the Burials Act of 1852 closed burial grounds in central London on health grounds. The 'mount' in the name comes from a raised area known as Oliver's Mount thought to have been used as a vantage point by Cromwell's army during the Civil War. The street was first built in 1720–40. The houses were modest, perhaps because the parish workhouse lay along the south side. The workhouse was extended over the years but ultimately demolished in 1886, by which time the 1st Duke of Westminster was rebuilding the street. Look for the fine 'decorated Gothic' Church of the Immaculate Conception, built in 1844; it is now a listed Grade II building.

Beside the church a slender garden opens out to a wider area, enclosed by tall buildings but offering a hidden retreat for those in the know. People who work in the area find the serene garden much to their taste in the middle of the busy working day. The tree canopy, mostly supplied by majestic old London plane trees, offers seclusion from the surrounding buildings. As an enclosed site the garden has a microclimate of its own, which allows foreigners like the Australian mimosa (*Acacia dealbata*) to thrive beside some dawn redwoods (*Metasequoia glyptostroboides*) from south-east China. The tender Canary Island palm (*Phoenix canariensis*) is a real rarity in London; it survives here near the far hardier Chusan palm (*Trachycarpus fortunei*). Beneath the trees, laurels, hollies and camellias do well on soil that is dry as well as shady. Adding to the unexpectedly exotic feeling are several Versailles planters holding feather palms (*Jubea chilensis*) in summer.

Left A secluded path meanders through the greenery of Mount Street Gardens, a refreshing interlude in the heart of Mayfair.

ST JAMES'S PARK

SW1

The oldest of London's Royal Parks, St James's Park covers 90 acres and has the Mall as its northern boundary, Birdcage Walk to the south, the Queen Victoria Memorial at the western end and Horse Guards Road on the east. It is first recorded as an area of swamp, regularly flooded by the Thames and Tyburn Brook and attached to St James's Hospital, a hospice for leper women. In 1532 Henry VIII acquired the land for deer coursing and duck shooting and built St James's Palace on the site of the hospice.

Over the centuries, other monarchs have made their mark. Elizabeth I hunted here. James I improved the water supply and established a menagerie (which included crocodiles and an elephant, watered with a gallon of wine every day) and an aviary, remembered today in the name Birdcage Walk. Charles I made minor improvements – and it was across St James's Park that he walked to his execution on 30 January 1649. Charles II, Versailles in mind, had the park completely redesigned, and the former swamp made into a long formal strip of water. When given some pelicans by the Russian ambassador, he enlarged the aviary; there are still pelicans there today, heavily cruising the lake. Another familiar name, Pall Mall, originates from that time, when land on the north side of the park was used for the King's favourite game, a kind of boules-cum-croquet named pell mell.

Under George IV the whole area was reshaped by John Nash. It is basically Nash's layout we see today, with limestone 'rockery', flower beds and trees, criss-crossed with paths and rest areas. The 'natural' lake was added in the mid-nineteenth century. The lushly canopied Duck Island is today is connected to the parkland. Duck Island Cottage was built in 1837 for the Ornithological Society of London and now houses the offices of the London Historic Parks and Gardens Trust.

The charming lake walk, beneath trailing willows and massive plane trees, weaves among the clamour of exotic waterfowl. From the bridge that crosses the lake, there are superb views of Buckingham Palace, the skyline of Horse Guards Parade and the London Eye. The bridge has been much used in spy films as a (highly unlikely) meeting place for undercover agents.

It was in Queen Victoria's reign that the royal family made Buckingham Palace their main London home, and in the early twentieth century the fashionable walk of the Mall was widened to become the famous processional route that it is today. Lined by London plane trees, it leads from Trafalgar Square, through Admiralty Arch, to the front of the Palace. To one side is St James's Park and on the other are the famous Nash terraces, the St James's Palace and then Green Park. As the Mall reaches its end, encircling the gilded Victoria Memorial in front of Buckingham Palace, it is bounded by flower beds that are always superbly planted with spring bulbs or summer bedding, often red, white and blue.

GREEN PARK

SW1

Refreshingly simple in design, Green Park is – as its name suggests – a greensward beneath a green canopy. Legend has it that when Queen Caroline, wife of George II, discovered

Page 80 Left, top: Whitehall looking like a fairytale castle in the early morning light. Left, middle: Duck Island Cottage is lushly planted with herbaceous flowers. Left, bottom: nonchalant pelicans preen themselves beside the lake. Right, top: the Horse Guards ride past the Old Admiralty, blazing with autumn colour. Right, below: summer planting in beds around the Victoria Memorial.
Page 81 Left: the London Eye seen from St James's Park, at sunset. Right, top: the wall of the Old Admiralty is famous for its thick covering of red vine in autumn. Right, middle: an early autumn stroll along a walk in St James's Park. Right, bottom: the Becontree Brass Band play on, despite summer rain.

that he regularly stopped to pick flowers from the park *en route* to visit his mistresses, she ordered that the park be grassed over. Rather disappointingly, there is no real evidence for this. But however it came to be, the adjacent hustle of Piccadilly and Constitution Hill is countered by this most restful of colours, with no flaunting flower beds to interrupt the calm. Only in springtime, when gentle carpets of daffodils and crocus colour the ground, or in autumn, when the canopy warms with coppery golds, is there any change of pace. For this serene quality the park is a great favourite with tourists and those who work locally.

It was not always so. Once this site was largely marshland, a place where the Tyburn Brook flowed through meadows towards St James's foetid swamp and the river. Enclosed for hunting land by Henry VIII, it was twice fortified, first by supporters of Mary I and then by Parliamentarians during the Civil War. Charles II created a formal deer park, criss-crossed with footpaths beneath plantations of trees, which made it an ideal spot for highwaymen and footpads.

It also became a focus for duelling and eventually, under the aegis of George II, for military parades. It was at this time that the first performance of Handel's *Music for the Royal Fireworks* took place in the park, to the accompaniment of rockets and cannons. Later, in George IV's reign, the park proved a perfect launching ground for hot-air balloons.

The Queen's Walk along the northern boundary, once a promenade for fashionable London, was planned by Charles Bridgeman for Queen Caroline. Today some of its former glory is recaptured when those who receive honours from the Queen are seen walking along the Broad Walk that crosses the centre of the park with their families in all their finery, from

Right Beneath the tree canopy in St James's Park the light is luminous after rain.

Buckingham Palace through the exquisite gilded Canada Gate along a direct path to the Ritz Hotel for a celebratory lunch.

The Ritz was built in 1906 at the north corner of the triangular park. Near by was the famous 'In and Out', the Naval and Military Club. Along the Queen's Walk are the Palladian Spencer House and the classically inspired Lancaster House, with Clarence House, home of the Prince of Wales, hidden behind. In the south-west corner is the rat run of Hyde Park Corner, visually overpowered by the grandeur of Decimus Burton's Constitution Arch and the Duke of Wellington's Apsley House, which has the remarkable address of No. 1 London. The southern boundary of the park, Constitution Hill, is said to have been named from Charles II's habit of taking regular 'constitutionals' along this route, walking his famous spaniels.

Today the fine stretch of gently sloping grass covers an area of 53 acres and has almost a thousand trees, with London planes, lime, poplar, oak and horse chestnuts dominating and small groups of hawthorn, silver maple, Indian bean tree and walnuts dispersed around the park.

VICTORIA EMBANKMENT GARDENS
WC2

Stretching along the river, on either side of Hungerford Bridge, the Victoria Embankment Gardens are tranquilly screened from the rushing traffic by greenery. It is a pity, though, that the river has to be so hidden from the gardens. Only a tunnel taking traffic below ground, as proposed by architect Lord Rogers, could remedy this.

The Embankment was a necessity, a fine feat of engineering built in the 1860s by Sir Joseph Bazalgette on reclaimed

Left Big Ben towers over a colourful bedding of primulas in Parliament Square.

riverbank mud flats to protect London from the tidal surges of the Thames and to provide space for the Underground, the sewers and other services. The new wall had to be 20 feet/6 metres above the high-water mark and a further 14 feet/4.5 metres below low-water level. It was lined with plane trees, which have now attained the gravitas required for such a site. Imposing Victorian buildings followed, including Scotland Yard, Whitehall Court and the Savoy Hotel. The walk along the Embankment is very fine, with views of the London Eye. It passes Cleopatra's Needle, the real thing from ancient Egypt, now quietly decaying in London's pollution, despite having survived for nearly four thousand years.

The gardens thread along the Embankment, edged by more magnificent plane trees. Designed by Alexander Mackenzie, they are mostly simple areas of lawn, protected from the road by carefully chosen shrubs and dependent for interest upon unusual specimen trees such as a golden Indian bean tree (*Catalpa bignonioides* 'Aurea') and a Judas tree (*Cercis siliquastrum*). Featured everywhere are scattered statues of the famous, including the translator of the Bible William Tyndale, and opera librettist W.S. Gilbert. Look also for the York Watergate near the foot of Villiers Street, built in 1626, which indicates where the shoreline then was.

In spring and summer colourful areas of bedding add decoration, and featured plants such as cordylines manage to look modern and Victorian at the same time. There is also Sir Arthur Bryant's secluded lily pond, which has attractive marginal plants including flag irises and hostas.

VICTORIA TOWER GARDENS
SW1

On the south side of the Houses of Parliament there is another green area separating people from traffic but this one is beside the river and offers some wonderful views from a relatively quiet and green site. Triangular in shape, the gardens also present a fine view of Victoria Tower and are often used for televised political interviews. They are equally famous for the cast of a superb Rodin sculpture, *Six Burghers of Calais*, which was placed here in 1915, having been removed from the Place Richelieu in Calais, where it commemorated the burghers' heroism at the town's surrender to Edward III in 1347.

In the centre of the garden is a colourful ornate Gothic fountain, once sited in Parliament Square. This is another memorial, to the social reformer Sir Thomas Fowell Buxton, acknowledging his role in the emancipation of slaves in the British Empire. A bronze by A.G. Walker of the suffragette Emmeline Pankhurst salutes the emancipation of women.

WESTMINSTER ABBEY
SW1

The historical site possibly dates back to the time when a Saxon church was built upon what was then Thorney Island. By the time of Edward the Confessor, there was a Benedictine settlement here, later ratified as a fully fledged Benedictine monastery. This established a monastic school, later Westminster School, which still operates from the site today. Since the crowning of the Norman William I in 1066, with very few exceptions the kings and queens of England have been crowned in the abbey. Westminster personifies the strength of the centuries-old link between the Church and the Crown.

The abbey is surrounded by gardens and yards which themselves have links to this long history. In the eleventh-century College Garden, one of the oldest continuously cultivated gardens in England, medicinal herbs were grown for the monastery. It is 1 acre square and now has a fine central lawn with views of the Houses of Parliament. There is a manicured small knot garden with four well-worn apostle statues against the fourteenth-century walls.

The little cloister garden is quite different, being compact and enclosed by the darkly vaulted cloisters. The visitor's attention is drawn inwards to the central fountain lit from the sky above. Many people find the small scale appealingly intimate and a great contrast with the grandeur of the abbey. Another enclosed garden, St Catherine's Chapel Garden, is not open to the public.

CHESTER SQUARE
SW1

This is a modest but intimate and serene private square, in its character typical of the Victorian period. The 15 acres were enclosed by the Grosvenor estates in 1828 and were laid out by Earl Grosvenor and Thomas Cubitt about ten years later. The fine church at one end, St Michael's, faced with Kentish ragstone, was designed by Thomas Cundy.

Left The statue of George V in front of Westminster Abbey, silhouetted by the setting sun that shines through the windows of the Chapter House.
Above There is a fine contrast between the spacious main cloister and the intimate Little Cloister of Westminster Abbey.

Some of the original trees remain, such as the huge planes, and in 1997 the garden was completely refurbished in period style, based on the Ordnance Survey of 1867. It is now a beautifully cared-for prize-winning garden with shrubs and herbaceous perennials. Spring bulbs and flowering cherries provide colour, followed by flowering shrubs such as fragrant white philadelphus. Rope tiles edge the borders in true Victorian fashion and yew hedges enclose the rose gardens.

The address has had associations over the years with many distinguished residents, including Mary Shelley, begetter of Frankenstein, and the poet Matthew Arnold, who, as parents often do today, eventually moved away to obtain better schooling for his numerous children. Two prime ministers have resided here: Harold Macmillan and Margaret Thatcher. The violinist Yehudi Menuhin had his home here, as did Lord Sieff, co-founder of Marks and Spencer. The square has royal associations too: Queen Wilhelmina of the Netherlands had her secretariat here during the Second World War. The garden is open on London Squares Day.

ECCLESTON SQUARE

SW1

Built by Thomas Cubitt in 1828 and named after the Duke of Westminster's estate at Eccleston, Cheshire, this square too has had its share of famous inhabitants, including Matthew Arnold (again) and, from 1908 to 1911, Winston Churchill. But for people with a passion for plants, the treasure is the central garden. Since it took the garden in hand in 1980, the Garden Committee, under the guidance of the horticultural writer Roger Phillips, has created a garden full of colour, using shrubs such as camellias, daphnes, philadelphus, hydrangeas and mahonias, and fragrances that waft across the square.

Above Looking west through spring cherry blossom in Chester Square towards St Michael's Church.

During his travels, particularly in China, Roger Phillips has collected seeds, some of which he has successfully germinated for the garden. Of these, roses in particular can be seen mixed with other shrubs and climbers, such as the large flowering light pink climber *Rosa* 'Belle Portugaise' from California, the small creamy-yellow flower trusses of *Rosa banksiae lutea* and China roses. The national collection of ceanothus grows here, over seventy species and cultivars. Some are evergreen, some dusty blue, some intense blue and some quite luminous pale blue; they flower at different times of the season. *Ceanothus* 'Delight', a deep blue, is a particular favourite. Overhead are some unusual flowering trees, including the foxglove tree (*Paulownia tomentosa*), the dove tree or handkerchief tree (*Davidia involucrata*) and the tulip tree (*Liriodendron tulipifera*).

As the garden is a shared space, the 3 acres are divided into smaller units, each with its own character. The committee also maintains a tennis court and a play area for children. Recently a gardener has been employed by the residents and with the assistance of garden enthusiasts she maintains a very high standard. The well-known Inchbald School of Garden Design resides in the square and its students are very fortunate to have access to the garden. This lushly planted paradise is quite unexpected in a city centre and shows what can be achieved. It can be visited twice a year under the Yellow Book scheme and on London Squares Day.

Right A damp day in summer when the ceanothus are in bloom in lovely Eccleston Square.

HISTORY AND HORTICULTURE

CHELSEA AND FULHAM

HISTORY AND HORTICULTURE
Chelsea and Fulham

Chelsea Physic Garden, Chelsea Royal Hospital, Fulham Palace, The River Café

During the late seventeenth and eighteenth centuries, as collectors brought back new plants to Europe from abroad, there was a great swell of learning in botany. One of the botanical gardens that benefited from the new discoveries was the Chelsea Physic Garden, which was to become a world leader in the collection and classification of plants. Another beneficiary was the ancient garden around Fulham Palace, into which many rare plants were introduced in the late seventeenth century. Both gardens profited greatly from the generosity of plant collector and philanthropist Sir Hans Sloane, who not only supported the Physic Garden financially but also distributed over eight hundred plants from his travels in Jamaica to these two London gardens (as well as to the Oxford Botanic Garden).

The mood of the ancient garden at Fulham Palace is tranquil. Once a complex of courts, orchards, gardens and fishponds, it is now a simpler place with a delightfully neglected enclosure inside the walled garden. The adjacent Bishop's Park, once part of the grounds, has been separated to make a long narrow riverside walk, peacefully secluded beneath an arching avenue of trees.

Today the Chelsea Physic Garden continues to display medicinal plants and to study the medicinal value of plant material. Its research programme includes systems for dealing with disease. The quest to collect and learn continues for horticulturists and gardeners today – as can be seen each year at the world-famous Chelsea Flower Show, held by the Royal Horticultural Society in the grounds of the Chelsea Royal Hospital. Many new hybrids and species are on display and there are exhibitions that concentrate on educational and scientific interest. The stunning floral displays in the marquee and the small gardens designed for the show indicate exciting directions in the art and craft of gardening – not only new looks and trends but also the revival of previous fashions. For example, as England's climate becomes warmer, exotics have come back into fashion. Ecological concerns, too, necessitating new approaches to familiar situations, have invaded the horticultural world.

The grounds of the Royal Hospital are in addition home to a delightful 'garden within a garden', Ranelagh Gardens. Also in this part of London, a haven of tranquillity of a different kind is the contemporary garden of the River Café, where visitors to the restaurant may sit outside on a summer evening beside the river in a simply designed rectangular garden that provides fresh vegetables and culinary herbs for the table.

CHELSEA PHYSIC GARDEN
SW3

In the second half of the seventeenth century, with the opening up of the Americas and the West Indies, plant collecting and exchange grew apace. The Chelsea Physic Garden, known originally as the Apothecaries' Garden, was founded in 1673 by the Society of Apothecaries, on land they had leased by the river; it was intended as a repository for some of these discoveries and a training ground for herbalists, where they could study their *materia medica*. Today the 3.8 acre site, one of the oldest botanic gardens in Europe, continues to be noted for rarities and its collections of plant species.

The garden has survived all the different developmental pressures imposed over three hundred years. This is largely thanks to the shrewd vision of its early patron, Sir Hans Sloane, the remarkable man whose great collections provided the basis for both the British Museum and the Natural History Museum. In 1722 Sir Hans, who was Lord of the Manor of Chelsea, transferred the garden by deed of covenant to the Society of Apothecaries in perpetuity: whatever the vagaries of 'progress' and the value of the land, it could never be sold and would continue as a botanic garden. The deed of covenant can be seen displayed in the garden.

When the Embankment along the River Thames was raised in the 1870s to avoid flooding, the garden lost its lovely river frontage and high brick walls were needed to enclose the site. These have become an asset, for they established a warm micro-climate. As a result, unexpected but large and healthy trees

Pages 90–91 The marshmallow pink cherry blossom of *Prunus* 'Kanzan' makes a vivid contrast with the warm red brick of the Hospital for Women in Dovehouse Street.

Page 93 *Echium pininana* from the Canary Islands, growing from a mass of *Tanacetum praeteritum* in the Chelsea Physic Garden.

Left A grass walk through the family order beds in Chelsea Physic Garden.

from around the world dominate the garden: among them the Asian wingnut, the American hickory and honey locust, the Mediterranean cork oak; and also the largest olive tree in Britain, which, after the hot summer of 1976 produced 7 lb/3 kg of olives (served with pride at Physic Garden drinks parties).

Today this rare and delightful garden gives enormous pleasure. Although the site is not large, the aim of the garden is to cover many facets of gardening, so there is a lot crammed in and a lot to care for. The visitor needs time to explore the variety and riches on offer. It may suit you to follow the historical walk to see groups of introduced plants associated with key figures in the history of plant collecting such as Philip Miller, Joseph Banks, John Lindley, the Victorian curator Thomas Moore and others.

Aquatic plants grow in the pond, tender and exotic plants in the glasshouses and a fern collection still thrives in the cool Victorian fernery. Laid out in a central position are systematic order beds where plants are ranked in rows according to their botanical family (as, for example the *Ranunculaceae* or buttercup associates), or other botanical groupings (as with the monocotyledonous beds for grasses, palms, irises, lilies and similar plants).

Sections are given to useful plants. For example, in the Garden of World Medicine are medicinal herbs from cultures as diverse as China, North America, Australasia and Africa. There is a collection concerned with perfumery and aromatherapy where rose, iris, jasmine, myrtle, mint and citrus flower. There are plants used for dyes such as madder, indigo and woad, and elsewhere edible fruiting plants, including apricots, grapes, figs and berries of many kinds. The garden continues to supply material for botanical research.

Right The oat-like inflorescences of the giant feather grass (*Stipa gigantea*).

CHELSEA ROYAL HOSPITAL
SW3

Like the Hôtel des Invalides in Paris, the Royal Hospital was the idea of a king, Charles II, who established the hospital for war veterans in 1682, in an elegant building by Sir Christopher Wren. At the time its gardens swept down to the river with parallel rows of trees. Today the busy road of the Embankment runs between.

Ranelagh Gardens

Today, a magnificent wide avenue of London plane trees separates the open area in front of the mansion from a leafier, quiet and secluded part of the park known as Ranelagh Gardens. These were built over the former house and garden of Lord Ranelagh, who lived there in 1690, and they run along the east boundary of the Royal Hospital. Initially, in the eighteenth century, these pleasure grounds were arranged in a formal style and were a place for the fashionable to be seen. Redesigned in the nineteenth century, the gardens are now gentler, with a more relaxed rural character and serpentine paths that weave around undulating ground. Densely planted groups of shrubs beneath huge old trees give way to open banks of grassland, with spring bluebells and foaming cow parsley. The resident Chelsea Pensioners have full use of the sunny spacious grounds.

Chelsea Flower Show

Each year, usually in late May, the Royal Horticultural Society holds one of the most famous garden shows in the world on the 1 acre site of the Royal Hospital grounds – a 'must' for the

Left Looking along Royal Avenue towards a storm brewing over Chelsea Royal Hospital.
Right A scene in the marquee at the Chelsea Flower Show.
Pages 98–99 The stands in the marquee display a vast range of plants. Here are lilies, lupins, snapdragons, delphiniums and spiky blue eryngiums with oriental poppies. The small picture on page 99 bottom left shows one of the gardens specially designed for the show.

horticultural calendar. A marquee is filled with the very best of garden plants, including exotic displays from around the world. Here there might be pyramids of apples, collections of hybrid lupins, recreations of tiny rockscapes for alpines or huge arbours and pergolas for roses, old and new. Specialists show beside amateurs and local authorities next to enthusiastic societies, and every year there are new things to see. Medals are awarded upon the skill of display as well as the quality of the plants. Special areas are given to education – a matter of great importance to the Society; white-hot updated horticultural information is available; and advice can be sought from professionals. There is nothing quite like this show anywhere else.

Outside the tent are gardens that look mature but are designed and built only for the show, which lasts for four days. Many are traditional, some flagrantly contemporary. Some display allegiance to other cultures. Some create a theatrical set piece and others try to emulate nature. The knot gardens of a French château might be next door to a garden showing the simplicity of cottage gardening in New England; elegantly minimalist designs with spare planting may be adjacent to an English meadow, lush with grasses and rich native flora; or the contemplative discipline of a Japanese garden might be seen contrasting with rows of magnificent date palms flown over especially for the show, to create an Arabic paradise. Some modern images reveal the beautiful and practical qualities of materials like steel, glass and concrete, while other gardens use recycled materials such as crumbed rubber, glass chippings and 'distressed metals'. Judging these show gardens is a serious matter and the use of plant material is always of prime importance. Gold medals are coveted.

The Royal Horticultural Society was founded as the Horticultural Society in 1804, over Hatchard's bookshop in Piccadilly, by a group of gardeners and botanists. Regular meetings were held at the rooms of the Linnean Society; an experimental garden was made at Edwardes Square and a nursery garden in Kensington. The show title 'Royal' was bestowed in 1861 under the patronage of Prince Albert. The early RHS Flower Shows were held in the gardens of the Inner Temple (see page 46). In 1913 the show was moved to Chelsea, and, with interruptions only during the two world wars, it has been held there ever since.

FULHAM PALACE
SW6

From the eleventh century to as recently as 1973, Fulham Palace, beside the River Thames, was the summer home of the bishops of London. As luck had it, several of the bishops were keen horticulturists, so the garden has a distinguished history.

Even before the garden was established the land had been worked for centuries, as farmland, grazing meadow and orchard. A Saxon moat once enclosed buildings and surrounding land, but the palace as we know it today was built in Tudor times. It is now a museum, owned and run by the local authority, with English Heritage looking over its shoulder.

The ornamental garden was created by Henry Compton, Bishop of London from 1675 to 1713. A biography written shortly after Bishop Compton's death refers to him as having a 'great Genius for Botanism' and 'an esteem for all those who were anything curious in this sort of study'. His famous collection of 'Exotick' plants began with the dispatch of a colleague, a botanist from Oxford, to Virginia. Among the first plants sent back for the palace garden were a dogwood (*Cornus amomum*), the spice bush (*Lindera benzoin*), sweet bay (*Magnolia virginiana*), sweet gum (*Liquidambar styraciflua*), the scarlet oak (*Quercus coccinea*), a dwarf sumach (*Rhus copallina*) and the maple *Acer negundo*.

Right An enormous ancient wisteria, heavy with flower, encloses the Victorian knot garden in Fulham Palace garden.

The garden remains renowned for its 'foreign' trees. An ancient evergreen oak (*Quercus ilex*) and black walnut (*Juglans nigra*) from that time still exist today. Other 'exoticks', including the Indian bean tree (*Catalpa bignonioides*), the Atlas cedar (*Cedrus atlantica* Glauca Group), the Chinese paper bark maple (*Acer griseum*) and the Mediterranean tamarisk (*Tamarix × tetrandra*) have been added in recent years.

Other features of interest include an eighteenth-century walled kitchen garden in which grapes and fruit trees were grown, and a Victorian knot garden for herbs and botanic beds.

The garden as a whole is intensely romantic: it has an air of being not quite in control, as if nature is poised to make a

Above A cloister of huge plane trees in Bishop's Park alongside Fulham Palace garden.
Opposite Artichokes and courgettes grow in containers in the River Café gardens.

comeback. Wonderful huge old wisterias wind their rustic way around the lushly thick Victorian knot garden, while ruined glasshouses cling to the old brick of the walled kitchen garden. The orchard inside the walled garden is now a 'savannah' dotted with recently planted old varieties of fruit trees, and it makes a perfect secluded spot for family picnics.

Adjacent to the park and part of the original estate is the Bishop's Park, a lovely river walk, and the Warren, now separate and the site of thriving allotments.

THE RIVER CAFÉ
W6

Beside the Thames, the River Café has a small simple garden that works within the geometry of the enclosing converted warehouses. A square courtyard, emphatically defined by narrow beech trees (*Fagus sylvatica* 'Dawyck'), is paved around the perimeter with stock and blue engineering bricks that link with the buildings. Within is a sunken, softly banked grassed square that protects visitors from the wind off the river.

Wind-proof pampas grasses (*Cortaderia selloana*) line the front and architectural plants such as figs and angelica add structure to the design. Fresh culinary herbs and vegetables are grown for the restaurant in pots and metal containers, including the odd experiment such as the magenta-toned New Zealand tree spinach (*Chenopodium giganteum*).

REGENCY RESPLENDENCE AND THE NORTHERN HEIGHTS

REGENT'S PARK, HAMPSTEAD, HIGHGATE AND FINCHLEY

REGENCY RESPLENDENCE
AND THE NORTHERN HEIGHTS
Regent's Park, Hampstead, Highgate and Finchley

*Regent's Park, Primrose Hill, Hampstead Heath, Parliament Hill Fields, Golders Hill Park, The Hill,
Fenton House, Kenwood House, Waterlow Park and Lauderdale House, Highgate Cemetery,
Highgate and Queen's Woods, Alexandra Palace, Avenue House Arboretum*

Apart from two small hills, Cornhill and Ludgate Hill, separated by the river Walbrook, the City of London is generally flat, spreading out along the flood plain of the Thames Valley over a layer of clay and outwashes of sand and gravel deposits. Further north, however, there is a gentle ridge of low hills that has become known as the Northern Heights. Here the gradient on slippery clay is such that – except for the small villages of Hampstead and Highgate, a few hamlets and the odd farm – little building was attempted until mid-Victorian times. Even then the greenness remained relatively free of development until a rush of Edwardian speculators, encouraged by better roads, set about covering some of the area with stucco and red brick. Nevertheless many open heaths survive, most famously Hampstead Heath. The area also includes the gardens of houses such as Kenwood and The Hill.

A large part of the charm of many of the places on the ridge lies in the views over London. In most cases, the prospect includes St Paul's Cathedral, in accordance with the St Paul's Heights Code, initiated in the 1930s by Godfrey Allen, then Surveyor for the Cathedral. Allen observed that the mighty domed building, intended by Wren to be visible from all over London, would quickly be obscured by the growing city unless strict building regulations were put in place to ensure that the dome would always be visible from key viewpoints. As buildings became larger the rules were extended to form the Strategic Views Policy. Today, although St Paul's is dwarfed by ever more massive towers, sightlines like that from Parliament Hill are still clear.

A view that could be admired from Primrose Hill until the nineteenth century was that shown in a drawing of 1616 by Nicholas John Visscher, looking across the River Thames, over the Globe Theatre and the original St Paul's Church to the distant hills studded with windmills. Today Victorian development conceals it and, although there is still a fine view, all eyes tend to turn south to look over the grand spaces of nearby Regent's Park, built in another era, an age of elegance when nature was kept in its place.

Distinguishing all the various landscapes are trees: some remnants of ancient woodland in the wilds of heathland and forests, and others planted over the last two hundred years, as were those in Avenue House Arboretum and fine specimens in such notable green spaces of north London as the grounds of Alexandra Palace, Highgate Cemetery and Waterlow Park.

REGENT'S PARK

NW1

Once part of the ancient Forest of Middlesex, and subsequently a royal hunting forest, Regent's Park is still owned by the Crown and, including Primrose Hill to the north, covers 472 acres. This large open space has survived a tortuous history dominated by self-interest, greed and commercial need.

The story began when Henry VIII enclosed the ancient woodland for his hunting. Over the following centuries it repeatedly came under threat as monarchs and Lord Protector alike sold off leases. By the late seventeenth century it was largely let off in smallholdings and during the eighteenth century these farms supplied hay and dairy produce to most of London.

In 1811 the Prince Regent, intent upon making London a place of style, commissioned the architect John Nash to plan a grand neoclassical scheme that pivoted upon Piccadilly Circus. A sweeping processional route was built to connect Westminster and St James's Park with an encircled space to the north that was to become the Regent's Park. Nash intended to develop this land as an upmarket housing estate with crescents and circuses providing elegant villas for the rich. But money and time ran out and fortunately this part of the concept was only partly fulfilled.

Instead we have a splendid park, planned as a circle within a circle and wrapped around from east to west by superb stucco terraces of large houses, with smaller intimate hamlets such as Park Village East and West. The northern perimeter, bounded by the Regent's Canal, connects the open parkland with the slopes of Primrose Hill. From here it once looked outwards to the rustic charms of the hill villages of Hampstead and Highgate.

The inner circle is now Queen Mary's Garden, with wide herbaceous beds, a sunken garden, a romantic lake with waterfall and rocks, as well as an open-air theatre for summer Shakespeare and a popular boating lake. Most of all, this site is justifiably admired for Queen Mary's Rose Garden, where a comprehensive collection of roses is encircled by tall posts supporting swagged ropes festooned with ramblers and climbers.

There is an old botanic garden, the Regent's College Botany Garden, which has been semi-restored and is occasionally open under the Yellow Book scheme. One of the best-known and oldest zoological gardens in the world also lies within the northern perimeter of the outer circle. The zoo, laid out by

Decimus Burton, was opened in 1826. Here, a 'Web of Life' exhibition demonstrates ecosystems and biodiversity, and Thames Water has sponsored a Water-wise Garden, showing ecologically interesting habitats for city gardeners. The zoo runs an important breeding programme for endangered species.

Not everyone knows about the 'secret garden' at St John's Lodge, just off the inner circle. Here, several circular enclosures, one large and the others smaller, are connected by a central line of symmetry through an elegant metal arch that focuses upon the Lodge. In the large garden blue-purple *Lavandula* × *intermedia* 'Grappenhall' edges old shrub roses and white campanulas. One of the smaller gardens is encircled by tall pleached limes with massed golden *Rosa* 'Graham Thomas', infilled with *Alchemilla mollis*, white philadelphus and yellow variegated-edged hostas with inserts of blue flowers.

Much of the rest of the park remains generously spacious, with spreading grass studded with many fine specimen trees.

PRIMROSE HILL
NW3

Almost an extension of Regent's Park, the tranquil green mound 206 feet/62 metres high that is Primrose Hill offers a splendid panorama over London. There are vistas over London Zoo and Regent's Park towards the low rises of Kent and Surrey in the distance. Landmarks can be seen from the City to Westminster, including the television mast of Crystal Palace and the London Eye. Very early in the day, lions can

Pages 104–105 Early morning calm near the boating lake in Regent's Park. The British Telecom Tower can be seen in the distance.
Page 107 A flowering crab apple tree before classical figures on a house in Nash's Cumberland Terrace, in Regent's Park.
Left Looking south after a rain shower on a summer evening in Regent's Park to a group of narrow-leaved ash trees (*Fraxinus angustifolia*).

Page 110 Top: spacious areas of grass studded with trees characterize Regent's Park. Bottom left: the Regent's Canal cuts through London Zoo, near Lord Snowdon's aviary. Bottom right: swans and a distant heron roam unconfined.
Page 111 Top left: a line of pink-flowering cherries in front of one of Nash's terraces. Centre left: in the 'secret garden', arches of climbing plants frame the view of St John's Lodge. Bottom left: the gilded gateway at York gate leads to Queen Mary's Rose Garden. Right: swags of climbing roses cling to thick rope.

be heard roaring, and wolves howling in the zoo below – an odd sound today but reminiscent of the past when the densely thicketed hill was a hunting ground with wolves, deer, game and wild boar.

Primrose Hill has a restive history. Used for demonstrations, duelling and military manoeuvres, it was rarely the green place of respite that it is today. An ancient prophecy in the sixteenth century by the 'witch' Mother Shipton stated that if London should ever completely surround the hill, the streets would 'run with blood'. In the four hundred years since then the dire warning has been well and truly tested. In 1678 a mysterious death caused havoc when Sir Edmund Berry Godfrey, a coal merchant and a Justice of the Peace for Westminster, was found murdered in a ditch below the hill, 'transfixed with his own sword'. This became the talk of the taverns and coffee houses. It was said that one Titus Oates had passed Godfrey documents proving that plotting was afoot to murder the king, Charles II, and replace him with the Catholic Duke of York. This was mere rumour but it suited the establishment to fan the anti-Catholic flames, and three servants of the Catholic Queen, Green, Berry and Hill by name, all highly unlikely suspects, were set up as conspirators and duly hanged at Tyburn. In consequence, Primrose Hill was for a time commonly known as Greenbury Hill.

On a happier note, Primrose Hill probably owes its more familiar name to the primroses that grew on the warm southern slopes in early spring. The grassy hill is crossed now with tarmac paths and lit with old-fashioned converted gaslights. Much of the grass is kept trim but there are wilder areas with long meadow grass. Hawthorn clumps dot the mound and quiet pastimes like kite flying and family picnics have replaced the dramas of history.

Left A summer evening on Primrose Hill, looking west.

HAMPSTEAD HEATH
NW3

Like Richmond Park south of the river, Hampstead Heath is an astonishing survival, having never been enclosed. But, unlike Richmond Park, it pays no obeisance to royalty: this common has always been for commoners.

Here are 790 acres of rolling grass, wild meadows, dark woodland, ponds and marshes, all linked by official and unofficial paths. These wild slopes are only four miles from the heart of the City, and ringed by the densely populated suburbs that grew from the old villages of Hampstead, Highgate, Golders Green, Kentish Town and Gospel Oak.

West Heath, Sandy Heath and Parliament Hill are part of the old wilderness and new additions like the tamed Golders Hill Park (see page 117), the disciplined garden of the Hill (see

page 117) and the sweeping formality of the Kenwood estate (see page 121) are included within the boundaries. Another area, the lush greenness known unexcitingly as Hampstead Heath Extension, ringed by Wildwood Road and Hampstead Way, has also been added. Families, dog walkers, horse riders, cyclists, birdwatchers, strollers and ramblers can 'attack' the heath from below, or from the ridge between Hampstead and Highgate.

Much of the distinctive character of the heath is due to the underlying soil. The whole of the heath could be described as a sandbank, formed over 40,000 years ago by a vast river bringing outwash from as far as the West Country and depositing it in southern England. Much later more detritus was added by glacial outwash from the last Ice Age that reached as far as Finchley. Impermeable London clay lies beneath it all. Over the millennia, rivers such as the Fleet have gouged out valleys and formed the lumpy terrain of the heath. Apart from the main ridge, there are on the heath two other large mounds that are

Above Hampstead Heath in low evening light, the view west over Highgate Pond.

still topped with sand. One is Parliament Hill and the other the Tumulus, which is romantically – but probably erroneously – supposed to be of neolithic construction.

Water is plentiful on the heath, sometimes as a natural spring but often in unlikely places, without stream or spring as source. Pools have formed where depressions, often man-made, have filled with water. Sandy Heath is very uneven, because of the commercial extraction of sand for building in Victorian times. Because the sand is very fine, with a high lead content, it pans as effectively as concrete, retaining water in shallow pools.

Natural springs reputed to have medicinal properties made the heath famous in the early eighteenth century, when people came to take the waters; there are reminders of the spas in names such as Flask Walk and Well Walk. Wealth accrued and fine houses like those in Church Row were built. The gentry stayed and the village never looked back. The heath is surrounded by watering places of another type: the old and famous pubs, all established in the seventeenth century. They include Jack Straw's Castle, named after one of the leaders of the Peasants' Revolt, the Bull and Bush, the Spaniard's Inn, the Flask in Highgate and the more intimate Holly Bush in Hampstead.

The Vale of Health at the western side of the heath is an eighteenth-century hamlet reputed to be a place free from disease, but probably originally named the Vale of Heath.

On the summit of the ridge is Whitestone Pond, once a watering hole for passing drovers. It is 443 feet/135 metres high. A string of ponds on the southern slopes are regulated to provide separated bathing for men and women. There is also a model boating pond and a pond that has been set aside for ecological purposes. These wet areas are a magnet for wildlife, and visiting birds and waterfowl find sanctuary on rafts in the water.

Left Looking east across Highgate Pond and the heathland towards the mass of trees near Millfield Lane.

host insects and small animals as well as plants, gradually establishing an ecological balance. As a source of information on natural history, Hampstead Heath was treasured as early as the late sixteenth century when John Gerard, author of the *Herball*, researched plants here.

The romance of the heath as a haunt of highwaymen such as Dick Turpin catches the imagination, but much of the fascination of the area is due to the people who lived in Hampstead and Highgate villages. The poets William Blake, Alexander Pope, John Keats and Percy Bysshe Shelley have strong connections, as did the ballerina Anna Pavlova, whose house is now a museum. The tradition continues today and many a famous figure from literary and artistic London can be seen striding the heath.

Having withstood many attempts at development, the main heath was finally saved for the public in 1871. That Hampstead Heath continues to exist in its present form is due to the efforts of vocal and powerful groups that prevent it from being tamed into parkland and see that there are no misguided attempts to prettify it with floral gardens.

Although seemingly wild, much of the heath is managed. The geological and ecological variety makes this quite a complicated job for the rangers. Parts are thought to be remnants of the ancient forest: for example, South Wood, behind the Kenwood ponds, has sessile oaks and wild service trees that indicate ancient woodland. In Sandy Heath pines grow on knolls of sandy soil with golden gorse below, and pockets of rhododendrons. A totally different atmosphere is created by a formal avenue of lime trees along the boundary path and another site where groups of blue cedars have been planted, and are now surrounded by green bracken and magenta willow herb. Much of the undergrowth elsewhere is naturally thick with holly, blackberries and nettles. Some areas of woodland still show where the medieval demand for timber once scarred the heath, depleting whole areas.

There are many sun-filled glades, particularly since the great storm of 1987, which felled many ancient trees. Some of these spaces are being left alone to regenerate naturally and are fenced off as Sites of Special Scientific Interest. Dead tree trunks

PARLIAMENT HILL FIELDS
NW5

Parliament Hill is the southern spur of Hampstead Heath, acquired for the public in 1889. At 320 feet/96 metres it is higher than Primrose Hill. From here can be seen a wonderful panorama that stretches from the great towers of Canary Wharf, over the erratic glittering blocks of the City, and westwards to include the British Telecom Tower and the Palace of Westminster, backed in the blue distance by Shooters Hill, the Crystal Palace and the North Downs; the elegance of the London Eye now adds a further dimension.

Above Windy Parliament Hill is a perfect spot for kite flying.

Various explanations have been put forward for how the hill acquired its name – one being that the Catholic conspirator Guy Fawkes arranged for his followers to have a gallery view from here of the Houses of Parliament ablaze. When the plot failed the audience was rounded up.

In the seventeenth century the fields were open pasture. Now they are gently undulating grassland, inviting at the weekend impromptu team games, such as football and Irish hurling. The hill is also known as Kite Hill after the activity that provides the main summer fun. This is replaced in winter by sledging, even skiing, if the snow is thick enough. Below the hill there are more sports at an athletics track, tennis courts and a lido.

GOLDERS HILL PARK
NW11

Adjacent to Hampstead West Heath, this park is quite different, being mostly formally arranged, although there is a wild part that was once the grounds of a large eighteenth-century mansion and was landscaped by Humphry Repton. It was re-modelled in Victorian times with the aim of including naturalistic planting, thereby going against the fashion of the day for organized bedding. During the Second World War, the house succumbed to the Blitz and the logic of the garden layout is now lost. Most of the 36 acres are given to sweeping mown grass, studded with remarkable trees such as the dawyck beech (*Fagus sylvatica* 'Dawyck') and the Turkey oak (*Quercus cerris*). Towards the heath the landscape changes dramatically to become shaded wild woodland. In this transition area there is a deer and animal enclosure, mobbed by children in summer.

Higher up the hill is a small water garden with a meandering path and audaciously arched bridge, from which can be seen

Above Exotic flowering plants, such as the brugmansias seen here, are planted out every year in the walled garden of Golders Hill Park.

highly colourful exotic ducks – a delight to little children. In spring primulas and flag irises edge the water, with small azaleas adding brilliance and mounding rhododendrons a secretive air.

The older generation loves the walled garden, formerly the kitchen garden of the house. It is noted for the carnival brilliance of the bedding. Dramatic subtropical exotics are brought out, too, for the summer season, including bananas (*Musa basjoo*) and the hardier fan palms (*Chamaerops humilis*), even sometimes agaves. Radiant cannas have a supporting role, followed later by dahlias, which reign until autumn. Sometimes missed by visitors is an ornamental 'orchard' of cherry trees that is entrancing in spring when the ground is covered with daffodils.

THE HILL
NW3

Enclosed within the rural seclusion of the Northern Heights is one of the most unlikely and hidden gardens in London. The Hill is a large sprawling house – once the home of Lord

Leverhulme, then a nursing home and now flats – with an outstanding Italianate garden about ¾ acre in extent. Restored recently by the Corporation of London, it is well worth exploring.

This period piece, designed by Thomas H. Mawson between 1906 and 1925, with terraces, colonnades and pergola walks, reaches out as if cantilevered, a man-made promontory over the steep slope of Hampstead West Heath. The long colonnaded walks have 'domed' crossings and 'tented' arbours along their progress, all with places to sit and wonder. The main axial route ends with a large brick-built belvedere that faces a superb panoramic view of Harrow-on-the-Hill and surrounding areas.

Above Sharp midday shadows define the pillars of the great pergola walk at The Hill.

When this part of the garden was completed, the area to the north-west of the house became the next challenge. The site was divided by an old right of way and Mawson devised a bridge to connect the upper terraces with this lower formal garden. Here is a long rectangular tranquil lily pool. The sloping lawns are immaculately mown, and shrubs and flower beds are well cared for. Above, the colonnades run along the southern boundary with elaborate stepped access as part of the design. On the south side, slightly incongruous below the main pergola and next to the woods, is a herb garden that was added recently.

It seems unlikely that visionary extravagance on this scale will be seen again so close to London.

FENTON HOUSE
NW3

The National Trust property in the village of Hampstead includes a seventeenth-century house that nestles in a walled garden of 1½ acres. You can find it by following the warren of narrow roads and passages that climb uphill from the village to the fine gates and walking through an avenue of robinias to the main entrance. The architect of the house is unknown. In 1793, it was bought by Philip Fenton, a merchant, and this is how it acquired its name. Inside is a remarkable collection of early keyboard instruments, including a harpsichord once played by Handel.

The frontal formality continues in the side garden with a narrow path between clipped standard hollies, which leads to the lower levels of the garden. These are treated as garden 'rooms', screened from each other by thick yew hedges. Beds edged with box are planted for year-round interest and blaze with herbaceous plants in summer. There is a brick-paved sunken rose garden, reached by charming small circular steps. Notice the wall planting,

Right Looking towards elegant Fenton House through a clump of blue agapanthus in flower in the back garden.

with many Viticella clematis among roses and wall shrubs. The atmosphere changes when, following the gravel walk, you reach an enchanting small orchard, which in spring is carpeted beneath the blossom with fritillaries and narcissi. Beyond is a vegetable plot where flowers for the house are also grown.

KENWOOD HOUSE

NW3

The estate around Kenwood House was partially designed by Humphry Repton in the eighteenth century, after Robert Adam had transformed the original modest brick house into a fine wide mansion. Repton aimed to mirror the elegance of the new house by setting it in a landscaped park.

Left The view looking over the lake towards the white mansion of Kenwood House and its orangery is probably little changed from Repton's day.
Above Sunlight touches the wind-stirred trees in the lower part of the Kenwood estate.

The main road was moved further from the house and a drive made with mounding rhododendrons and large horse chestnut trees to conceal the front entrance. To the rear, the terrace was extended to revel in the magnificent view of the City – Adam had declared that he could see boats moving on the Thames from here. Repton felt that a partially landscaped woodland enclosure would create the illusion that the estate reached down to the river. To this end he proposed that some trees should be felled in South Wood below the house. But today the trees have grown, most of the view of the river is hidden, and the vista from the terrace is only of the grass slopes that sweep downhill to the two lakes of the pleasure grounds. The sham bridge beside one of them already existed, placed there by the owner, the 1st Lord Mansfield, but it was not to Repton's taste (I rather agree with him).

It seems that Repton asserted that the gardens to the west side of the house should be more intimate, with sinuous paths hidden within flowering shrubberies creating 'variety, incident

WATERLOW PARK AND LAUDERDALE HOUSE
N6

Waterlow Park is at the eastern end of the Northern Heights, running down beside Highgate village. Given into public ownership by Sir Sydney Waterlow in 1889, the 27 acres of parkland offer glimpses of a wonderful prospect of the City – although it always strikes me as odd that where the best views should be, at the top of the park, the land is terraced to make tennis courts. This could imply that those who laid out the landscape thought that active pursuits should have priority over quieter, more reflective pleasures; but probably it was sheer convenience that led the design. Below the courts, the park sweeps magnificently downhill, following the natural contours of the land. Firm pram-worthy paths swerve around the steep grassy slopes.

Around the open spaces are fine specimens of copper beech, limes, oaks, maidenhair trees and cedars of Lebanon. Some are originals from the old estate. This is a treasured park that offers much to plant-lovers. There are rose beds and the area around the lake is especially attractive in spring when azaleas and irises are in flower, and in autumn when Japanese acers come into their own. There are large sculpted logs on the ground to amuse young children, and a small aviary is another draw. The lower ponds provide a sanctuary for other, wilder birds. All year round, the trees and water tempt colonizing wildlife from the adjacent virtual nature reserve that is Highgate Cemetery.

Within the park is Lauderdale House, a Grade II listed building of 1580 with a walled garden of its own. Some exotic trees, including ginkgos, honey locusts and tulip trees, and wide magnolias tower above. Lower down, where formal garden meets parkland, are lushly planted herbaceous beds.

and surprise'. One of the surprises is at the side of the house, where a path from the front drive leads through a long and narrow ivy-clad tunnel to reveal the full theatrical effect of the picturesque landscape below. In the flower garden on this side, in front of the shrubbery, sculptures by Henry Moore and Barbara Hepworth emulate the magnificent art collection inside the house, which includes work by Rembrandt, Vermeer, Lawrence and Gainsborough.

In summer, open-air orchestral concerts are held on a canopied stage and music drifts across the water in the gathering darkness of evening. The large audiences sit on the grass or in deckchairs but this is neither Brighton beach nor Glyndebourne: Kenwood has its own relaxed style.

In 1925 a member of the Guinness family, the Earl of Iveagh, bought the house and in 1927 he gave it and the grounds to the nation, adding 32 acres to Hampstead Heath. It is owned and managed by the Corporation of London and English Heritage.

Above Looking from Swain's Lane, down the steep hill of Waterlow Park, over sweeping areas of mown lawn and rough-cut wilder grass.

HIGHGATE CEMETERY

N6

During Victorian times, when densely packed church burial grounds had begun to threaten the health of the living, large spaces were allocated for cemeteries to be built in suburban London. The inner city became encircled by new burial grounds, known as the 'magnificent seven', built to take the increasing overflow. The burial business prospered and cemeteries were planned like mini-city developments, with wide main avenues, narrow 'side streets' and miniature buildings built for generations to share. Tasteful chapels were included to fulfil all non-secular needs and as a statement of social rank.

Of all these new cemeteries Highgate Cemetery is the most famous, both because of the famous people buried in its 37 acres and for the extraordinary architectural fantasy of the tombs. The grand entrance is spacious enough for funeral cortèges headed by plumed horses drawing the hearse and followed by professional mourners. On one side is the Anglican Chapel and on the other the Dissenters' Chapel, ensuring that all were catered for. These Grade II listed buildings have traceried lancet windows, above which are battlemented parapets. As for the tombs, architectural style is uninhibited: they are high Gothic, classically Greek or ancient Egyptian, with pillars that are Doric, Ionic, Corinthian, Romanesque or even barley sugar twists, standing beside Egyptian obelisks or Celtic crosses. The main path that leads though all this is the Egyptian Avenue, which is entered by an arch with papyrus columns upon a plinth of lotus – an upside-down theme that is repeated throughout the cemetery as a mark of respect for the dead.

The scheme culminates in the Circle of Lebanon, a circuit that is gouged out of the natural hillside and lined on the outer and inner concentric circular walls with dank mausoleums. The path between them encircles the centre where a mature cedar of Lebanon grows. On the crest of the natural rise of land are more large family catacombs, built into a long terrace from which the views are magnificent, but in the interest of safety this is not accessible at present. All other routes wind around smaller, ivy-clad tombstones, beneath mature planted tree specimens and thickets of wild saplings, growing up to the light and in some cases supporting tottering gravestones.

The cemetery was consecrated in 1839. It was an instant success as a place where the fashionable could be 'seen' visiting and from the early days it was a tourist venue. As a result, it became a hugely popular place for burials, and a mere twenty years later an extension was built across Swain's Lane. The original cemetery became known as the Western Cemetery and the new area the Eastern Cemetery. An old tunnel connects the two cemeteries. Coffins were lowered by hydraulic means from a chapel in the Western Cemetery to pass along the tunnel beneath the road, and collected on the eastern side.

The Eastern Cemetery, which is always open, is famed as the place where Karl Marx is buried. His enormous sculptured head dominates everything. The grave is rarely without an awed bystander but whether this is for idealistic reasons or because of the overlarge scale of the black head is a question that provokes thought. Other distinguished notables here include the novelist George Eliot and the actor Sir Ralph Richardson.

In the Western Cemetery lie Charles Dickens' family, scientist Michael Faraday, Carl Rosa, founder of the Opera Company, the novelist Radclyffe Hall and many other celebrities of their day. Of the two cemeteries, it is the more romantic, having an additional charm that would have deeply shocked the Victorians, for the magic comes from neglect. Despite the loving and sensitive care of the Friends, it is a hopelessly overgrown, beguiling wilderness. Wild flowers mingle with garden escapees; ivies blanket the ground and make small trees by climbing up tall tombs; ferns grow beside bracken. The place is a perfect nature reserve, with areas of dark shade, open

meadow grass and damp wetland. It is a twitcher's heaven where many bird species breed, alongside foxes, hedgehogs, butterflies and insects. It is also wonderfully peaceful because the public can only visit at scheduled times. Age, assisted by mosses and lichens eating into the stone, has weathered the dwarfed architecture, begetting a fantasy that is pure theatre. I remember walking through the snow one winter, when it was as if a fantastical set had been designed by Leon Bakst.

But despite its romance and roll-call of distinguished names, going right up to modern times, the cemetery has a slightly threatening air. I confess that I would find it a bit frightening if I were alone. I would pay money not to be buried there; although when it came to it I don't suppose I would be bothered.

Above The sunken circular 'ravine' around the catacombs of the Circle of Lebanon, beneath the ancient canopy of the cedar that is older than the cemetery. Beyond is the gleaming Portland stone tomb of Julius Beer.

HIGHGATE AND QUEEN'S WOODS
N6

These two quiet woodlands, vestiges of the old Forest of Middlesex, became the property of the bishops of London, then were handed over to the Corporation of London in late Victorian times. Although surrounded by densely populated suburbs, and with sensibly hard-surfaced paths, they retain closely packed large trees. And the wild service tree grows in both woods, an indication of their ancient history.

Highgate Wood has rather lost the feeling of natural woodland because it is a thoroughfare for the tube station and much used for dog walking. Apart from elder, holly, hawthorn and rambling blackberries, the undergrowth tends to be sparse.

In the less-used Queen's Wood the slopes are greener, with winding paths that lead down to an old paddling pool. Oak trees vie with hornbeam, making the woodland quite dark, and little groups of silver birch struggle for the light. The wood makes a habitat for bird life, with insects and small mammals thriving in an undergrowth of wood anemones, violas and foxgloves.

The green corridor of the Parkland Walk travels through the woods, following the abandoned railway line that ran to Alexandra Palace from Finsbury Park. This narrow meander is now a lushly verdant nature reserve and butterflies have a penchant for it.

ALEXANDRA PALACE
N22

This monument to Victorian pride has suffered from two burnings, the first within only sixteen days of its opening in 1873 and the second in 1980. However, the 'people's palace' has been partially restored and is now used for exhibitions,

Right Queen's Wood in golden autumn, with a thick carpet of leaves.

conferences, garden shows, cat, dog and rabbit shows, ice skating and liquid hospitality. It was from here that the BBC first transmitted television in 1936 and it still has the mast at one end of the long building. Standing high on the ridge of the Northern Heights, the building is visible for miles – a northern rival to the Crystal Palace. From here there are superb views over north London to Kent and the far North Downs.

The parkland of 220 acres is a green hillside, mostly in front of the palace, that drops steeply down to Hornsey, with specimen hollies, ash trees, horse chestnuts, copper beech, nothofagus and silvery poplars. Once Victorian pleasure grounds, it is sometimes used for concerts, although no event compares with the Victorian pyrotechnic melodrama *The Last Days of Pompeii*, produced here in 1888. Then there were temples, palaces, slaves, soldiers and priests, all meeting their end with the eruption of Vesuvius as the scenery went up in flames.

Here today the old racecourse below the wide terrace is no longer and no hot-air balloons have been launched for years. Gentler pursuits like kite flying and picnicking are now more usual. Even the flower beds have been grassed over. But there are still firework displays, now computer controlled and more extravagant than ever. More fun is available to the rear of the palace, where there is a boating pond, a children's playground and a dry ski slope.

To the east a compact nature reserve thrives quietly down the hill, despite the proximity of the busy railway line and adjacent Alexandra Palace station. It has all the benefits to wildlife of a pond, long meadow grass, woodland copses and a secluded atmosphere. This is a wild and pretty place for accompanied small children and those who just need to feel that the countryside is near by.

Right Looking from the park below as a storm dramatically threatens Alexandra Palace and the television transmitter.

At the top of the hill another intimate area, but without wilderness appeal, offers enclosed pockets of seclusion. This area was once landscaped, being the grounds of a fine house, the Grove. High above the clutter of London, it was famous as a summer residence and was leased by aristocrats such as Lady Diana Spencer, daughter of the Duke of Marlborough, who in the eighteenth century spent a summer there painting in the grounds. An avenue of trees still stands, known as Dr Johnson's Walk. James Boswell writes, 'Mr. Johnson went with me to Beauclerc's villa [the Grove] . . . It is delightful, just as Highgate. It has . . . greenhouses, hot house, observatory, laboratory, chymical experiments . . . in short, everything princely.' The estate was added to the grounds of Alexandra Palace in 1863 and the house was demolished ten years later with the coming of the railway line. Open spaces created by former landscaping make the Grove a place to meet, to hear jazz on sunny Sundays and take part in other summer events that give it a strong community identity, making it quite distinct from the open sweep of the rest of the palace grounds.

AVENUE HOUSE ARBORETUM

N3

This romantic small (16 acres) public park has enormous charm. It was laid out in 1880 for Henry Stephens, known as 'Inky' from the family business; the original ink laboratory can still be seen in the house. The house and grounds were given to the local council in 1918.

The park still holds many of its original fine trees. There are over a hundred different tree species, some of them rare. Near the house a massive ancient weeping beech (*Fagus sylvatica* 'Pendula') is crushing an old wall but, supported by stilts, it lives on. There is a walk that starts on the left of the entrance and follows the perimeter of the park, looking out towards the central grassed area at a magnificent mature sweet gum (*Liquidambar styraciflua*). Passing between the magenta-flowering Judas tree (*Cercis siliquastrum*) and ancient English oaks, the visitor enjoys a view across the lawn of magnificent tree foliage. Note the contrast between the fluttering silver grey poplars (*Populus* × *canescens*) and the green oaks, limes and beech trees.

The path leads to a small enclosed area of brilliant orange, yellow and red azaleas, and turning right passes below more huge and interesting trees, including the Caucasian wing nut (*Pterocarya fraxinifolia*) and an eagle's claw maple (*Acer platanoides* 'Laciniatum'). Groups of conifers include deodar and Atlas cedars, with a wellingtonia (*Sequoiadendron giganteum*) from California, a pine from Bhutan (*Pinus wallichiana*) and a swamp cypress from Missouri (*Taxodium distichum*).

Look also for *Quercus frainetto*, an oak from the Balkans, the pin oak (*Q. palustris*) from the United States, *Sophora japonica* from China and many other long-distance travellers. Fine examples of European trees thrive here too, including food suppliers from our past such as mulberry, walnut and the compact shrubby quince (*Cydonia oblonga*).

There is an unusual walled garden, the Bothy, which is to be restored and eventually opened for the public. This is an intimate and romantic flowery garden around what is now a community and arts centre.

As some of the original treasure trove of trees have aged they have had to be removed, but the local authority is adding more and these are helpfully labelled.

Right Large blue Atlantic cedars frame an inviting view into the arboretum of Avenue House.

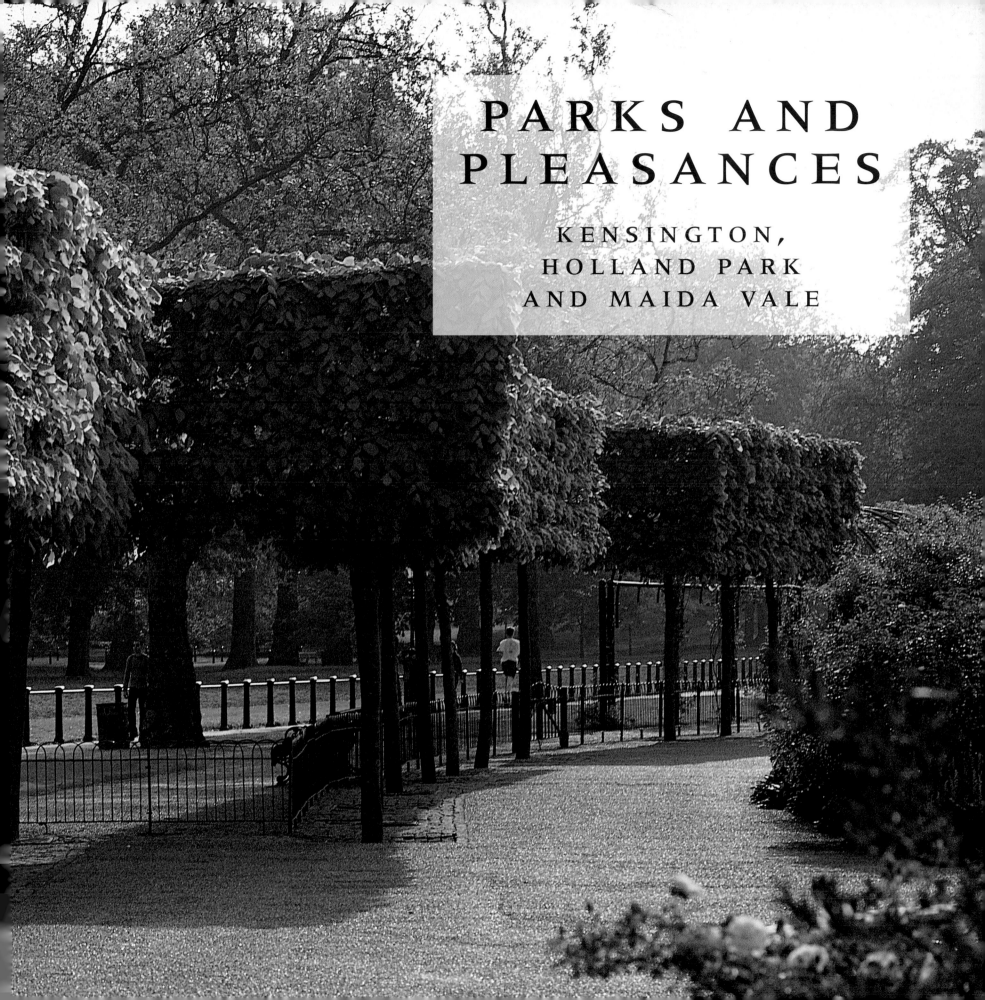

PARKS AND PLEASANCES

KENSINGTON, HOLLAND PARK AND MAIDA VALE

PARKS AND PLEASANCES
Kensington, Holland Park and Maida Vale

Hyde Park, Kensington Gardens, The Roof Garden, Holland Park,
Victoria and Albert Museum and Natural History Museums, Emslie Horniman Pleasance,
Meanwhile Gardens, Little Venice, Clifton Nurseries

Few cities of the world give quite as much space to nature as London does, for people to enjoy with their dogs and horses and birds, native and ornamental. The large green parklands of central London alter the pace of the fast-moving city. The rhythms of sound mutate from urgent to tranquil and textures change from hard to soft; the air clears and green replaces grey.

Most of the parks are green and flowing in design, reflecting the character of the British landscape. Grass, shrubs and huge trees create intimate verdant spaces or direct the eye along vistas.

Dominating both the parks and the streets of the city is the imposing London plane (*Platanus × hispanica*, syn. *P. acerifolia*). In summer it gives deep shade below and provides homes for sparrows, greenfinches, magpies and, of course, pigeons, plus many transients. In winter the flaking bark makes jigsaw patterns up the trunk, and the branches above are loaded by hanging baubles of burred fruits. The plane tree is a survivor: the branches can be cut back over and over again if necessary. It is abused above ground by atmospheric pollution and often below ground as well by repeated hole-digging for gas pipes, power lines, drains and cables, but it persists.

The large parks – Hyde Park and Kensington Gardens – were made for pleasure, with tastefully judged landscaping that was savoured at first by monarchs and their courtiers and eventually by everyone. Both of these parks have sweeping grassland with large trees and slowly flowing stretches of water, all cunningly managed to resemble the English countryside, as well as avenued perspectives, inviting walks and graceful pavilions.

The smaller and more formal Holland Park reflects a time when unnervingly unpredictable real countryside was kept out by walled boundaries. Now, when our efforts are to conserve threatened nature, the fashion is to introduce to these enclosed spaces 'nature areas' which are in their way as artificial as the knot gardens of the past. A section of Holland Park is one such area; so too are the woodland areas that contribute to the charms of Meanwhile Gardens and the Roof Garden in Kensington.

But the public also expects colour in the parks and the park authorities meet this demand in summer by providing immaculate bedding, in the manner that became fashionable in Victorian times. Wallflowers, forget-me-nots and bulbs are followed by pelargoniums, salvias, marigolds and gazanias, which are tidily framed by silvery dusty miller or exotic coleus. The effect is as if the ground were covered with rich oriental rugs. What some find gaudy others perceive as excitingly colourful.

HYDE PARK

W1, W2 AND SW7

Hyde Park is coupled with Kensington Gardens, the dividing line being the road that cuts from Kensington Gore, over the Serpentine Bridge to Bayswater. But the two parks are very different. Hyde Park, though a royal park, is essentially classless in character, relating to both the nearby commercial hustle of Oxford Street and the sophistication of Mayfair. In the north-east corner, where Tyburn gallows once stood, is Marble Arch and here Speaker's Corner reaffirms the park's democratic character.

It is worth studying the maps at the entrances to the park, for it is large – over 340 acres. The area was referred to in the Domesday Book as a wild place owned by the abbot and convent of Westminster. Later it became the property of the Crown and Henry VIII's hunting ground. Opened to the people by Charles I, the park has often been used for ceremony and fun. Military displays such as gun salutes on the Queen's birthday still take place here. The hugely successful Great Exhibition was held here in 1851, in the massive Crystal Palace, designed by Joseph Paxton. Sports such as wrestling, horse racing and morris dancing, popular in the past, have been replaced today by impromptu games of football, baseball and softball, with occasional outdoor pop and promenade concerts attracting huge numbers of people.

To the west, the Long Water of Kensington Palace Gardens flows into the Serpentine lake, passing beneath the bridge on West Carriage Drive, a Regency addition of 1826. In the next century, when cleansing methods were introduced to clear the sewage that contaminated so many of London's rivers and pools, swimming became possible. Initially this was confined to the early morning and to men only, but in 1930 George Lansbury established a lido for all, at all times, including the traditional Christmas morning swim, when on many occasions the ice had to be broken first. The lake is also popular for boating in summer. From the Serpentine Bridge the visitor can look over these activities towards a fine view of Westminster's towers and the London Eye.

Despite today's noisy, swirling traffic, the park is a peaceful retreat. Early in the morning the Horse Guards and others can be seen exercising their horses along the historic route known as Rotten Row, a name corrupted from 'Route du Roi', the king's ride.

In summer large expanses of grass make the park a place for sunbathing, picnicking and simply strolling. But the character is quite different in the north-west segment, where the Meadow, between North and West Carriage Drives, is quieter, even on hot days. Here the grass grows long, awaiting haytime. Many parks must have looked like this in pre-lawnmower days. The ground is gently undulating beneath trees that are mostly natives related to the ancient woodland. Here you can lose yourself in the countryside; with birds in the trees and butterflies in the tall grass, it is impossible to believe that London is all around.

Close by, hidden from the public, are a series of large greenhouses where the bedding plants for all the Royal Parks are grown. And there is an environmental centre for children near the old Police House.

Much of the park is flat and open to sunshine and here sunbathers, immodest or discreet, revel in the heat. But the magnificent tree canopies provide welcome shade as well. The original elms have gone but plane trees form long avenues and there are magnificent specimen trees such as copper beech, the tree of heaven, Caucasian wingnut, red oak, Indian bean trees, sumachs and magnolias. An enclosed garden south of the Serpentine is filled with flowers, particularly rose beds. And there is a wonderful scented summer stroll beneath a series of rounded arched pergola walks. The intimacy of the garden is reinforced by the fine boundary of pleached lime trees that make a stilt hedge.

At the time of writing, the competition for the proposed Diana Memorial Garden has been judged in favour of Kathryn Gustafson's design, based upon a ring of water. There are already voices of protest – it is impossible to please everyone and we are a cautious nation – and the maintenance costs are thought likely to be very high, but the park needs something strong and contemporary to represent the new era.

Pages 130–131 A stilt hedge of limes brings an almost French air to Hyde Park's rose garden.
Page 133 The bathing pool in Hyde Park, on this snowy day more popular with ducks than people.
Opposite Early morning riders in Rotten Row.

Pages 136–137 Hyde Park and Kensington Gardens have much to offer: a place for vigorous exercise or a quiet walk; borders where silvery stachys gleams among old roses; magnificent trees, such as the flowering horse chestnut shown here. Boating on the Serpentine is popular in summer; near the Serpentine Gallery refreshments can be taken in a temporary architectural fantasy; and people, as well as birds, enjoy the wide stretches of water.

KENSINGTON GARDENS
W2, W8 AND SW7

Kensington Gardens is one of London's most loved parks. It was originally the parkland surrounding Nottingham House, which was converted into Kensington Palace when William III bought it in 1689. Charles Bridgeman laid out much of the design in the early eighteenth century. It includes a wide footpath, the Broad Walk, that connects Kensington in the south to Bayswater in the north and which became fashionable for promenade and display. The West Carriage Drive established segregation from Hyde Park, but today the parks are inseparable because of the umbilical sweep of the Long Water, which flows into the Serpentine lake. The slim curve of the Long Water, originally the Westbourne stream, was controlled as a series of fishing ponds until, on the imaginative orders of Queen Caroline, wife of George II, these were linked together as the Long Water, to flow into the Serpentine in Hyde Park.

The Long Water begins below an ornate balustraded Italianate terrace, set out in 1861 by James Pennethorne. It is said that Prince Albert intended this to be modelled upon the Petit Trianon at the Palace of Versailles in France, but it lacks both conviction and glamour. A large pavilion and four pools, each centred on fine plumes of water, combine to make a dutifully formal geometric climax to the Long Water. The terrace and its buildings hide the pumping station, but I find the area grey and solemn and much prefer the light relief further along the banks where there are some wildlife areas, thick with tangled shrubs and trees. These contrast vividly with the ranks of limes and planes that make up the tree-lined allées and vistas so characteristic of the park.

Many of these avenue walks originally radiated from a levelled area in front of the palace, which is now the site of the

Above A fine walk through drums of clipped holly and bay focuses upon the elegant Orangery.

famous Round Pond. In fact, it is not truly round, being more ornate than a simple circle, but its open aspect and plantless surface have made it a draw for nannies and their charges as well as more grown-up children who share a passion for model yachts. The tall sails mingle with visiting swans and make silent progress as the wind dictates. Kensington Gardens will always be associated with children – partly because of the author of *Peter Pan*, Sir James Barrie, who lived locally and 'adopted' a family of impecunious boys whom he encountered there. Peter's statue by Sir George Framdon stands defiantly blowing his pipes, and he is rarely lonely.

West of Peter Pan, near the Orangery, is another draw for children. In 1852 the poet Matthew Arnold wrote 'Lines Written in Kensington Gardens'. Its myths and fairies have been brought to 'life' by Ivor Innes, who carved the famous *Elfin Oak* with brightly coloured elves, fairies and goblins emerging from the natural gnarled form of the long-dead trunk. The oak is next to the large Princess Diana playground, another draw for youngsters, complete with pirate ship. It was created to commemorate the Princess's love of children.

There is much more to enjoy in the park. The Sunken Garden, created for Queen Anne in 1722, has a Dutch flavour. It is planted first for spring, then for summer, with an eye to brilliant colour combinations, although what is explosively vibrant to one may seem brashly technicolored to another. Surrounding the rectangular garden is a dense hedge of pleached limes into which 'squints' have been cut. It is through these that the garden is best viewed. Visitors peep through to see three sunken tiers of radiant spring or summer bedding, planned like an ornate picture frame around the focal scene of a long rectangular pond, surfaced with water lilies.

Right A view of the spire of St Mary Abbots in Kensington, over the Round Pond.

Near by, the elegant Orangery of 1704 must not be missed. It is particularly attractive when approached from the south along a path lined with huge cylindrical holly and bay trees. Orange trees are set out on the terrace in summer, as was originally intended. Any one of three famous men, Sir Christopher Wren, Sir John Vanbrugh or Nicholas Hawksmoor, may have designed the building. Pause to take tea in the elegant room and admire Grinling Gibbons' carvings before setting off to view the front of Kensington Palace through the magnificent gilded Crowther Gates.

Then you may decide to follow the line of tulip trees (*Liriodendron tulipifera*), one of the earliest 'exotics' to be grown in England, and divert to the colourful Flower Walk and the gleaming Albert Memorial. This magnificent commemorative piece, designed by Sir Gilbert Scott, is unashamedly elaborate, a worthy acknowledgment of Queen Victoria's and the country's debt to the Prince Consort. A tall Gothic spire on a massive stepped plinth – surrounded by carved marbles representing the continents of Asia, Africa, Europe and America – crowns the enthroned gilt-bronze figure of the Prince.

There are new features in the gardens that are planned for a contemporary look. Each summer a large temporary summerhouse-cum-café is built beside the Serpentine Gallery near the bridge. The commissions for these structures are awarded to innovative architects and the results have been exciting. There have been pavilions designed by Zaha Hadid and Daniel Libeskind, and in 2002 Toyo Ito, with Arup, created a superb white, light and linear construction of glass, aluminium and air.

Top Looking through an avenue towards the Round Pond, with statue and snowman competing for attention.
Centre A view from the Broad Walk to the gilded gates of Kensington Palace, in autumn.
Bottom The young Queen Victoria is framed by a row of lovely hawthorn trees in flower.

THE ROOF GARDEN
W8

High above Kensington High Street in 1936–8 a garden was built covering 1½ acres of rooftop on top of Derry and Toms department store. Designed by Ralph Hancock as three distinct gardens surrounding the Rainbow Room restaurant, it is still unique in London for its spread, its ambition and its bravura. It survived the Second World War and the replacement of the old store in the 1960s by fashion shop Biba, which flaunted the flamboyance of its own era until it too closed. Now above more prosaic shops, and owned by the Virgin group, it is justifiably a Grade II listed garden.

The first area is the formal Spanish Garden with characteristic Moorish detail, such as ornate tiles and barley sugar pillars. A narrow canal divides the area and paving defines four immaculate lawns. Fan palms, vines and figs grow with silver-leaved Mediterranean plants and spiky New Zealand phormiums, supplemented in summer by flowering plants in terracotta pots.

The Tudor Rose Garden has old brick walls around small paved courtyards. The 'ground' is paved with patterns of brickwork edged with solid flagstones.

The third garden is based upon English woodland and includes a lake with cascades, bridges, trailing willows, exotic ducks and Chilean flamingoes. With the rustling leaves overhead, the winding walks through shaded or flowering shrubs, the ducks floating on their stream in the sky and the general freshness of woodland plants, it is utterly convincing. Only occasional glimpses through 'windows' in the wall confound the illusion.

Considering that the soil here, up on seventh-floor level, is nowhere deeper than 3 feet/1 metre and often less, the way this garden thrives is astonishing – and a great tribute to the thoroughness of the care and feeding programme.

Right From the elevated walk above the Moorish cloister the Roof Garden might appear to be at ground level – except that we are also looking through to the eighth-floor windows of the neighbouring department store.

HOLLAND PARK

W8

To my mind, the best way to enter the park is from Holland Park Avenue to the north. Here the natural look of the landscape makes an effective contrast to the grand stucco villas and elegant avenues of the surrounding area. The opposite entrance, from Kensington High Street, is more formal, being a straight hard-surfaced path along an avenue of trees leading beside the sports field and tennis courts towards Holland House, formerly the home of the Fox family, Barons Holland, and now owned by the Youth Hostel Association. The rural delights of the park are hidden behind the house.

This is a charming small park, only 55 acres in all, but with great variety to appeal to a wide range of visitors. It is a garden of contrasts, where authoritative geometry directs the eye along vistas or meandering routes to give inviting glimpses of pools and glades within woodland. The elegant Orangery, a habitat for art, is only a few steps away from decomposing old tree stumps, left as a habitat for insects and therefore birds. A chestnut walk and lime tree avenue contrast with woodland planted with oak, birch, lime, horse chestnuts and beech and thickly filled with an undergrowth rich in holly and ivy. All this is complemented in spring with daffodils and fragrant English bluebells. This woodland is also a small arboretum where trees like mulberry and pear attract butterflies and insects.

Wildlife areas are treasured. There is an ecology service which has a centre near the arcade, a remnant of the old house, that organizes a programme of events in the park. The ponds are particularly popular with families, who can see frogs, dragonflies, birds and butterflies, lured into central London by the lushness of the park.

Left In early summer the area near the Orangery of Holland Park glows with the rich colours of flowering irises.

More formal gardens have a different appeal. Here the brilliance of the azalea walk in late spring starts the flowering season. Irises, roses, herbaceous perennials and, for late summer, massed dahlias ensure continuous colour. Summer bedding is immaculate and an area for tender subtropical beds adds excitement.

One very distinctive area of the park is the Kyoto Garden, a Japanese garden planted with wonderful acers, elegant maples that have red, yellow and green foliage. Around the pool, carefully placed rocks and paths are exquisitely laid and accessible. A great favourite is the waterfall, crossed by granite-slabbed stepping stones that are a magnet for children, and many adults.

Above The Kyoto Garden in Holland Park, created by Japanese gardeners, is colourful all year, but autumn brings out the best in the maples.

The arcade, beside the Iris Garden and adjacent to the roses, is almost as much of a draw. Here are ramblings of wisteria and nostalgic murals of Victorian garden parties, painted in 1995 by Mao Wen, in which drifts of elegantly dressed ladies take a turn around the sunlit estate. Close by, the peacock lawn offers the occasional flash of quivering colour.

VICTORIA AND ALBERT MUSEUM AND NATURAL HISTORY MUSEUM
SW7

Of the fine museums built in South Kensington during Queen Victoria's reign, two have interesting gardens.

The Victoria and Albert Museum wraps around a spacious central courtyard, the heart of the museum. Once the theme here was vaguely oriental but in 1987, under the directorship of Sir Roy Strong, a bold decision was taken to alter the image.

People were fond of the existing flowering cherry trees and there were protests at the time – and even today the discontent rumbles on – because the formal design that replaced them was considered by some to be harsh and unsympathetic. It does have a grandeur that would suit a serious war memorial, but the simplicity is necessary and the geometry suits the Italianate façades of the courtyard; the basic sense of order fits well with the very elaborate architecture. Possibly there will be a call for change again when the Libeskind extension is built.

The layered design of the garden – known as the Pirelli Garden – is formally Italianate, with a central fountain. Lines of suitably columnar incense cedars (*Calocedrus decurrens*) have been chosen to emphasize the geometry. Opposing groups of Italian alders (*Alnus cordata*) create dappled shade, softening the understated design. This inner sanctum is a quiet space within an intensely Victorian building crammed with ornamental riches, and in summer it is a huge relief to those who are saturated with culture.

Across the road, the garden of the Natural History Museum is quite different. The theme here is nature and ecological balance – hot topics in today's world. This garden is managed by the Wildlife Trusts partnership, which is the leading British conservation charity.

About 1,000 trees and 20,000 wild flowers have been planted in a 1 acre site. One major objective is to provide visitors, especially children, with an insight into the study of urban wildlife, and there are interactive schemes that are altered according to the season. However, visiting has to be controlled because disturbance affects the research programme. Therefore the garden is open only for small groups, with guided tours throughout summer.

Above A glass sculpture by Dale Chihuly animates the simple geometry of the Pirelli Garden tucked inside the Victoria and Albert Museum.

EMSLIE HORNIMAN PLEASANCE
W10

This park for the people owes its existence to a local Member of Parliament, Emslie Horniman, who, recognizing that there was no place for children 'within a mile', in 1913 gave the land to the borough in perpetuity for 'the people of London as recreation ground'. He commissioned the architect Charles Voysey to design it and the result owes a lot to the period when Lutyens reigned. A very Voyseyan building marks the entrance to a 'secret' walled garden, screened from the road by high white walls, which are pierced at regular intervals by circular viewing windows. Inside is a central rectangular area, boldly framed by a typically robust timber pergola with a slim glittering moat of water beneath. The lushly filled beds of roses and flowering herbaceous perennials are thriving since a recent restoration.

Above left The undulating surface in the children's playground in the Emslie Horniman Pleasance is made of coloured recycled crumbed rubber.
Above right The large timber pergola in the sophisticated Voysey garden.

In the 1960s slum clearance offered the chance to expand the site and now there is a large open children's playground, which undulates enticingly and has a soft surface of resin-bonded, brightly coloured crumbed rubber, saved from recycled car tyres. Gates and fencing are designed with style and verve, being made from panels of perforated sheet steel with bright yellow wavy frames and railings. Altogether the playground is fun as well as child-friendly, a great contrast to Voysey's rather serious design. But, because the park is subject to heavy use, all the furnishings have to be strongly designed and the materials are quite as heavy and hardy as those chosen by Voysey.

The site includes a large platform that comes in handy during the Notting Hill Carnival as the perfect setting for the Steel Band Panorama, and there is a wide sweep of grass, crossed with winding paths made of concrete setts, coarse aggregate and sloping edges with flows of large pebbles set in concrete. The planting is bold – there is, for instance, a run of dramatic *Phormium tenax* along the inner metal boundary of the Voysey garden.

flagged with yellow irises offering sheltered edges. A spiral path of glassy aggregate securely set in a resin binder wends around the site, linking all parts. Heavy-set rail sleepers separate areas but lean obliquely, conjuring up associations with the wind and the sea. Everything is sturdily built – partly a realistic means of coping with heavy use but also implying that the park is important, that it is valued by the authorities, by the designers and by the users. It is here to stay.

LITTLE VENICE
W9

Many of the old rivers of London, such as the Fleet, were gradually drawn into the sewage systems and covered over. But new waterways in the form of canals were built to link the national canal network with the Thames. The London network is now known as the Grand Union Canal. The earliest section, built in the late eighteenth century, became part of a complex transport system that fell into disuse when the railways proved to be faster and more efficient.

These waterways often penetrate parts of London not visible from the roads and a trip on the canals is quite revealing. Buildings turn their backs to the canal, as when they were built it was the commercial highway, the motorway of the day, on which boats transported industrial goods such as coal; and the routes are lined with storage yards and industrial sites. Today people have a different attitude and houses beside the canals are sought after. Along the Regent's Canal expensive new mansions are being built, in the Nash style, to front the water – this in a neighbourhood that once insisted upon the canal being taken around the north of the park, where it had to be hidden in a cutting. Factory conversions and sophisticated

And there is a quiet garden, a sunken green space for plants and people – a contrast to Voysey's strong design that works well with his original bold concept of eighty years ago.

MEANWHILE GARDENS
W10

Popular and heavily used, this area along the Grand Union Canal throbs with life at Notting Hill Carnival time. In the shadow of the Trellick Tower, a skateboard surface offers a hilly uneven terrain – a contrast with the relentless geometry of high-rise buildings. Made originally in the 1970s but updated in 2000 with a powerful and thoughtful design, the linear park provides variety for all.

There are four main areas, each with distinct character. A grassed end with potential for young children is gently verdant, and has views through to the slowly flowing canal. A wooded garden encourages wildlife and has timber boardwalks, as if to invite the visitor to explore some native forest. The pond is

Above Graffiti enlivens the popular bike and skateboard bowl in Meanwhile Gardens.

developments like that at Paddington Basin on the Grand Union Canal attest the revised value of the canals.

Little Venice is a particularly lovely part of London. It lies amidst substantial Georgian villas, built in the early nineteenth century at Maida Vale, north of Paddington. The poets Robert Browning and Lord Byron once lived here and both called this the Venice of London, but the name did not really come into common use until after the Second World War. It is at the junction of the Grand Union Canal, built to connect with Birmingham, and the later Regent's Canal, which flows through Islington and out to the Thames at Limehouse.

When all commercial activities on the canal ceased in the 1950s people quickly saw the charm of this area. The canal is wide enough for permanent moorings of narrow boats and barges. Moorings are prized and the boats, gaily painted in bold identifying colours, are maintained to a high standard. Some of these treasured homes claim adjacent areas of towpath for their own. Boat owners sit out on their towpath gardens in summer beneath tree canopies, with 'boundaries' defined by their own rose-clad arches and evergreen plants. Everything grows in containers. There are climbers woven into the railings and a glut of pots filled with flowers from spring to summer. 'Roof gardens' drip with verbena, pelargoniums and petunias, with young hydrangeas in fancy containers resembling swans or even, in one case, a Venetian gondola. One resident, owner of the *Lady Venice*, has been here for twenty-five years and has regularly won the London in Bloom competition.

Waterbuses glide quietly along this endlessly interesting stretch of the canal, sliding through Maida Hill tunnel, passing the rural green spread beside Regent's Park and beneath Lord

Top This section of towpath at Little Venice has been commandeered by a permanently moored boat-owning gardener for his colourful flower display.
Bottom Gaiety rules at Festival time in the basin at Little Venice, when flags and canal art compete with the flowers.

Snowdon's aviary at London Zoo, turning left at the Cumberland Basin *en route* for Camden Lock. A trip on the Regent's Canal from Little Venice to Camden Lock is one of the most pleasant of London outings.

CLIFTON NURSERIES
W9

Established at the beginning of the twentieth century, Clifton Nurseries are found by walking through a narrow entrance between imposing cream stucco houses in the area of Little Venice. They are well-presented nurseries, crammed with goodies. The shop has useful information sheets, free to the visitor, on topiary, container plants, shade plants, ground cover plants and many other aspects of planting particularly relevant to urban gardens.

A wander around the plant displays is enticing. There are beautifully built glass-covered walkways as well as an enclosed section for indoor plants, with guzmanias, cacti, hibiscus and feather palms. A fernery holds dicksonias as well as smaller tender ferns and there is a great choice of containers, including traditional replicas and others made from modern materials. The gardener can find everything here, from trellis to garden furniture; from old obelisks to contemporary sculpture; from recycled *objets d'art* to minimalist art, as well as architectural salvage. And there is a garden landscape service. The staff are friendly and knowledgable, and whether you are buying plants or just visiting you can wander at will.

Left Eating *al fresco* in the shade of London planes, outside a pub in Maida Vale.
Right In summer narrow boats, barges and waterbuses, passing the moored homes, make the Grand Union Canal busy. This view shows the bridge at Warwick Avenue.

RETREATS

CHISWICK, BRENTFORD, ISLEWORTH AND EALING

RETREATS

Chiswick, Brentford, Isleworth and Ealing

Chiswick House, Chiswick Mall, Syon House, Osterley Park,
Gunnersbury Park, Gunnersbury Triangle Ecological Park

The aspiration to have a second home out of town, a country cottage for weekends and holidays, is not a new one. When the wealthy families of eighteenth-century London wanted to get away from it all they built or 'improved' imposing classical houses west of the city, at such locations as Chiswick, Syon, Osterley and Gunnersbury. They were close enough for it to be feasible to ride into town for the day or invite guests to enjoy lavish house parties, surrounded by exquisite pleasure grounds, with flower gardens, exotic trees, walled gardens and ambulatories that led to pavilions set by lakes or in woodland. The surrounding parkland often had vistas cut through for viewing, as at Osterley and Chiswick.

Such creations reflected the changing fashions in landscaping, from the formal classical geometry of the past to a newer, more relaxed style. There was a new conciliatory attitude towards nature, seen no longer as menacing wilderness but as beautiful and harmless enough to be brought into the park and artlessly managed as a form of art. The pioneer of this new art form was William Kent, encouraged by his patron at Chiswick House, Lord Burlington. Kent avoided the bonds of traditional formalism in garden design and, encouraged by Alexander Pope, pioneered a new romantic classicism of idealized nature. 'Capability' Brown, at first absorbing Kent's

training at Stowe, learning about the principles of composition using architecture with landscape, eventually moved towards a 'natural' free style of landscape with lakes, rolling pasture and woodland, still very structured but not in the classical Italianate style that had so influenced Kent.

Now the eighteenth-century country homes, which once brought so much pleasure to their owners and their guests, are not in the country at all. They have become part of the suburbs of London. Open to the public, they continue to bring pleasure by offering a taste of *rus in urbe*, the country in the town.

Today nature is as important in gardens as it was in the eighteenth century, but the balance is tipped towards the power of nature rather than the power of man, and our pleasure in nature is humbler. We delight in its charm, in its logic, by which the right conditions sponsor the right plants, and in aiding nature to find its ecological balance – indeed the delicacy of judgment required to do this has turned it into another fine art; and we fear not the wilderness itself but the possibility of losing it altogether. Playing a small but significant part in averting that tragedy is the Gunnersbury Ecological Triangle Park, saved from development by local action. It is now a reserve where nature holds sway, conserving within the city a piece of the country for which Londoners yearn, in the twenty-first as in the eighteenth century.

CHISWICK HOUSE
W4

Chiswick House is one of England's finest Palladian villas. It was modelled in 1725 upon Palladio's sixteenth-century Villa Rotonda near Vicenza. The 3rd Lord Burlington chose to build it not as a 'home' (he lived next door in a Jacobean house), but rather as a temple to culture, where he could display his books and paintings and enjoy entertainment in the form of cultural dialectics with his friends, who included Pope, Swift, Handel and Gay. For such a fine house the setting had to be a serious undertaking.

The 67 acre garden at Chiswick House shows some signs of the linear pattern-making of Charles Bridgeman, and Lord Burlington also involved Alexander Pope in the landscaping. But the garden is mostly the work of Burlington's protégé, the revolutionary landscape designer William Kent.

Lord Burlington and William Kent saw Chiswick as a garden in a transitional style. They were both greatly influenced by their travels and by the paintings of Claude Lorrain and Nicolas Poussin, in which the romance of classical antiquity was depicted by 'distressed' classical architecture and 'antique' sculpture was set in picturesque nature. At Chiswick they blended the *allées* of France and the classical formality of Italy with the new ideas of natural landscape, planned with artfully random groves and shrubberies. The concept of Arcady was developed through the formal simplicity of symmetry and straight vistas. There are radiating straight paths between yew

Pages 150–151 Chiswick House is framed by a graceful sweep of great cedars, supplemented by rows of classical urns.
Page 153 One of the radiating straight paths that were restored in the gardens of Chiswick House in the 1950s. Closely confined by yew hedges, they entice visitors to explore.
Left The classical Ionic temple, set in a turf amphitheatre around a small circular pool, looks much as it would have done to Lord Burlington over two hundred years ago.

hedges, randomly dotted with classical statues, including statues of Caesar, Pompey and Cicero brought from Hadrian's Villa at Tivoli. At the end of each walk the focal points become in turn a pivot for more radiating *allées*. They are intricately connected and draw the visitor on to explore further. Some vistas culminate theatrically in a semi-circular hedged boundary known as an exedra; others create prospects that terminate at an obelisk or urn. One path leads towards Wyatt's classical bridge of 1788. Or the visitor may choose to follow a path that leads directly to a circular pond, centred on a small obelisk and surrounded by a turf amphitheatre with an Ionic temple on the far side. In summer this magical place is filled with fragrant orange trees in tubs, arranged around the concentric terraces.

Kent's vision also included introducing nature into classical order, and a long serpentine lake was built to end in a cascade which, however, has never actually worked. Walpole, enthused, writes of 'the waving irregularity' of its curving banks, in which the 'gentle stream was taught to serpentine at its leisure'. Add to this Kent's dramatic use of light and shade, achieved by planting groups of trees so that shadows 'broke too uniform and too extensive a lawn' and here you see the beginnings of a new approach to landscape.

There is also a nineteenth-century Italian garden set with brilliant bedding. The designer was Lewis Kennedy, who had worked in France for the Empress Josephine. Joseph Paxton designed a conservatory to house the famous camellia collection begun by the 8th Duke, which is now much expanded. And at the eastern end of the garden is Inigo Jones' gateway, brought here in 1736 from Beaufort House in Chelsea. Around the house there are majestic trees, such as the huge

Right In a tribute to classical Roman gardens, stone figures are dotted around the formal areas of the garden at Chiswick House. Many are partially concealed as they slot silently into yew hedges.

cedars of Lebanon and a massive and rare specimen of the narrow-leaved ash (*Fraxinus angustifolia*).

Over the centuries, the garden has had quite a mauling, producing some major changes. Gardens are such transient things, and decisions on whether to excavate and thereby remove one period to reveal another are always controversial. But Chiswick House and its garden were inspired by Lord Burlington's visits to Italy, and this has been the governing factor in the recent restoration of the garden.

CHISWICK MALL
W 4

Near by, along the River Thames, is Chiswick Mall, where a very pleasant walk along the riverbank passes several superb old villas, some of which open their gardens under the Yellow Book scheme in April and June. The houses themselves are interesting, in particular Bedford and Eynam Houses. They date to the seventeenth century or earlier, but some have more recent façades. Occasionally the river floods over the road, temporarily removing some of the signs of the twenty-first century.

SYON HOUSE
TWICKENHAM, MIDDLESEX

Across the river from Kew lies the lovely estate of Syon Park, extending over 55 acres. In the fifteenth century there was a convent of the Brigettine order here. This was annexed by Henry VIII as part of his purge of the monastic houses and it was here that the king's fifth wife, Catherine Howard, was imprisoned before her execution in 1542.

Top Early morning light creates long shadows in one of the gardens beside the river in Chiswick Mall, in early summer.
Centre The same garden but late on an evening in spring when the magnolia is in full flower.
Bottom The river walk at Strand on the Green on the north bank of the Thames, facing Kew Gardens.

The present house was built in the reign of the child King Edward VI by the Duke of Somerset, Protector of the Realm. In 1594 Elizabeth leased it to the Percy family, later Dukes of Northumberland, who ultimately acquired the freehold. The house, today much altered, still stands in spacious parkland with water meadows, avenues, a wilderness garden, and magnificent native and exotic trees. The association with horticulture was established early, when William Turner, physician and author of the first serious English botanical reference book, *The Names of Herbes*, written in 1548, studied the herbs and plants growing in the rich alluvial soils of Syon. He lived across the river and regularly rowed over in search of medicinal remedies.

Above Beside the lake at Syon House, the aerial roots of swamp cypress (*Taxodium distichum*), technically pneumatophores and more colloquially 'knees', could be families of gnomes on a day out.

Early in the seventeenth century the garden was laid out with the formal regularity of the time, and had a walled kitchen garden and orchard. Later, lime tree avenues were added and a 'great fountain garden' was built in front of the house. Records show that at that time the orchard had 200 cherry trees, 100 apple trees and 6 mulberries (of which 4 ancient specimens still survive). Ramparts were extended to claim more of the water meadows and another wall, built in 1715, defined the Wilderness, a site for a collection of native trees and shrubs planted with random naturalness. But in 1739 a great frost destroyed many of the trees, including the lime avenues.

In the mid-eighteenth century, the whole concept of the garden was changed radically. The 1st Duke of Northumberland employed the fashionable leader of the new romantic style of landscape gardening, Lancelot 'Capability' Brown, to lay out the parkland that we see today. Much of the old formality was eradicated, although some traces of the avenues remain. Over a period of twenty years, from the 1750s to the 1770s, the garden was transformed into the Syon Pleasure Ground. A ha-ha was built to support the illusion, looking from the house, of an unbounded garden where lawn merged with wilderness. Old drainage ditches became long slim lakes, still beautiful today.

In the kitchen gardens a hot wall was built for vines and melons, and pineapple pits were added, to supplement the apples, cherries and pears that grew so easily. A 'botanic house', with light from above and sash windows, was built to house exotic plants. Beside it was a modish aviary. Eventually a menagerie of swans, geese, duck and guinea fowl added to the pleasures. In the associated tea room, the first tea plant in Europe flowered in 1773.

The nineteenth-century garden writer J.C. Loudon dedicated his book *Arboretum Brittanicum* to the 3rd Duke, who was his

Left The sublime dome of the great conservatory at Syon, though built of cast iron, is exquisitely light and airy.

patron and another passionate gardener. It was he who built the Great Conservatory as a replacement for the old botanic house. The appointed architect, Charles Fowler, designer of the Covent Garden market buildings, was inspired by Joseph Paxton and created a glass and metal building upon creamy Bath stone, partly resembling an eighteenth-century orangery but with a glass-domed conservatory. The dome housed tropical plants, such as palms, and the wings of the building held ranks of camellias on one side and orange trees on the other. Plant-hunting expeditions were sent by the Duke to every continent, to collect plants such as orchids. Advanced horticultural techniques enabled the successful growing of 'new' plants, including vines that were to become the foundation of the Australian white wine industry. At the Great Exhibition of 1851 Syon pulled off a great coup when they displayed the giant water lily *Victoria amazonica*, which they had propagated themselves. A distinguished book, the *Alphabetical Catalogue of Plants of Syon Garden*, published by Richard Forrest in 1831, listed the thousands of plants collected and growing at Syon.

The gardens were opened to the public in 1837 and the walk around the long lake remains a great draw. The trees, many very old, others rare, make a fine collection. On both sides of the lake are tall handsome swamp cypresses (*Taxodium distichum*) with characteristic knobbly roots rising above ground like small brown gnomes in the grass. Walking along the lake, the visitor has to duck to pass beneath a huge weeping Caucasian wingnut tree (*Pterocarya fraxinifolia*), whose heavy branches sweep to the ground where they root and start a colony. Other trees include zelkova, liriodendron, catalpa, eucalyptus, metasequoia and several varieties of pine, spruce and fir. Lower storeys include an old established medlar (*Mespilus germanica*) as well as quince (*Cydonia oblonga*) and strawberry trees (*Arbutus unedo*).

Despite the proximity of Heathrow airport, the atmosphere of the long lake is quietly tranquil. Mixed greens, softly textured willows and dramatic tree trunks establish the charm of this stretch of water. In spring, carpeting yellow daffodils and aconites, followed by bluebells, beneath blossoming cherries and fluffy white cow parsley, line the boundaries, bringing colour to the woodland. Yellow flowers of native water lilies float on the surface of the water and the golden spathes of the huge-leaved skunk cabbage (*Lysichiton americanus*) grow along the edge. The massive foliage of rhubarb-like *Gunnera manicata*, trailing willow branches and vertical swamp cypress are reflected in the sheen of the lake.

Other parts of the garden include another tree collection in the Wilderness, to the south-west of the house, and near to the Rose Garden, where alba, gallica, damask and moss roses flourish. But for me it is the grace of the trees that makes this a place to pause, to absorb the sense of space and to sit and view Kew gardens beyond the water meadows across the river.

OSTERLEY PARK
ISLEWORTH, MIDDLESEX

The park was enclosed in the latter part of the sixteenth century. In the eighteenth century the house (built by Sir Thomas Gresham) and the parkland passed to the Childs, a family of bankers who needed a country villa away from the toiling City, for weekending house parties. They employed Robert Adam to make substantial improvements. An enraptured Horace Walpole visited the house after Adam's classical colonnaded revisions and declared, 'It is so improved and enriched that all the Percies and Seymours of Sion must die of envy.' It is this remodelled house that is seen today, standing in Regency pleasure grounds with serpentine lakes. House and parkland stayed with this family until finally coming into the care of the National Trust in 1949.

The earlier layout of the grounds was very grand, with canals and avenues radiating from the house. All was swept away in

the late eighteenth century by the new fashion for 'natural' landscaping. But the great meadow behind the house does belong to the original Tudor period, hence the name Osterley, meaning western meadow. A contemporary painting shows that it is substantially the same as it was then, albeit now shortened to screen a modern housing estate. It is thought that the mounds of tree clumps in the meadow relate to the Tudor period, before the land was levelled.

The pleasure grounds, east of the house, were a focus for agreeable strolls, and two buildings by Robert Adam provided tranquil rest areas as well as winter protection for tender plants. The Garden House, completed in 1780, is elegantly semi-circular, with tall windows giving light to orange and lemon trees, which were wheeled out for high summer. The existing seats are replicas of the originals. The other building, a formal orangery, was destroyed in the Second World War. This was

larger and housed tender Mediterranean plants such as oleanders and myrtles. But the Temple of Pan still exists. Possibly the focal point for one of the original avenues, it is a classical Doric building, adorned with plaster reliefs that represent the arts and the sciences.

Closely associated with the Garden House is the flower garden where visitors took much pleasure. Now being restored to the style of the period, the planted beds are circular, oblong and oval. William Mason, who worked here from 1770 to 1790, planted herbaceous perennials, tender perennials, biennials and annuals together for summer effect. Notice how the plants are deliberately spaced to anticipate their full spread, with a surround of soil – very different from today's more casual

Above Cedars of Lebanon (*Cedrus libani*), some planted over two hundred years ago, cast wide shadows over the flat ground beside Osterley House.

overflowing bounty. Small plants are planted tidily around the edges with taller ones towards the centre; the gradation of height means that all may be seen. The Walled Garden near by, providing cut flowers for the house as well as food, was also a source of tender flowering plants. It was described by Walpole as costing as much as '£1,400.00 a year' to maintain. It is not yet open to the public.

On an expanse of flat mown grass between the house and the lake is a truly magnificent group of wide-spreading old cedars of Lebanon (*Cedrus libani*), one of which was planted in 1785. Cedars of Lebanon are frequently seen in the grounds of large country mansions of the seventeenth and eighteenth centuries (their association with the Bible lands added greatly to their attraction). There are other fine trees in the gardens including an ancient cork oak (*Quercus suber*) and in the pleasure grounds north of the house is a handsome oriental plane tree (*Platanus orientalis*), planted in 1755. Its lower branches sweep to the ground, with crimson summer fruits hanging like Christmas tree decorations beside last year's sepia-brown winter fruits. Regrettably, it is too close to a comely copper beech (*Fagus sylvatica* var. *purpurea*), but as even that was planted over 150 years ago it is now to late to do anything about it. There is an arboretum and pinetum on the site as well. When the Americans John Adams and Thomas Jefferson visited in 1786, they noted that 'exotic' evergreens were grown here, and in later Victorian times conifers and rhododendrons were added. Now there is a collection of North American plants and by the lake are four handsome swamp cypresses (*Taxodium distichum*) from the Mississippi.

Long routes around the estate reward the walker with fine views of the house and a chance to follow the curving line of the lakes and islands surrounded by a park of groves and native woodland. You can follow all this with an excellent tea in the original stable tea rooms.

GUNNERSBURY PARK
W5

This old parkland site of 186 acres has a fine history but is now suffering from some neglect, despite the efforts of the Friends of Gunnersbury: maintenance is very costly. Nevertheless, some restoration has started, like that of the eighteenth-century bathhouse. There are also plans, devised by the Gunnersbury Garden Project Committee, to rebuild a former Japanese garden, made by James Hudson in 1901; it is to be hoped that the committee's energetic fundraising and careful research will bring the project to fruition and that the elaborate pools and waterway systems will also be restored.

According to tradition, Gunnersbury acquired its name from Canute's niece, Gunhilda. It is thought that a mistress of Edward III, one Alice Perrers, lived here in the manor. By the sixteenth century it had passed through several families. A Palladian house was built in the seventeenth century by John Webb for Sir John Maynard, later becoming the summer residence of Princess Amelia, daughter of George II. It is thought that William Kent worked on landscaping the estate for her. The bathhouse too relates to this time.

The local authority, which now owns the site, has placed many clear information boards that explain the original layouts of the seventeenth- and eighteenth-century landscapes and show how they have been affected over the centuries. The greatest change came when the Palladian house was demolished in 1801, after which the estate was divided in two and plots were provided for several large houses. Ultimately, only two elegant neo-classical mansions were built, high up on the hill with commanding views. These now house an arts centre and museum, with a fine collection of paintings, maps and displays on historical and archaeological themes. The Rothschild family bought the estate in 1835 and employed Sydney Smirke to make alterations and build the orangery and the stables.

William Kent is thought to have designed the circular pond, now enjoyed by people and Canada geese. An elegantly simple classical temple stands beside it, reflected in the water on still days. This pavilion is a relic of Princess Amelia's time, when outings to take tea outside were one of life's garden pleasures. It was probably designed as an ornamental dairy.

On the lower slopes there was once a lake beside the orangery, but it was destroyed in the last war and it has not been possible to restore it. The rolling lawns are still there, sweeping down towards the site of the lake. Some beautiful and rare trees are planted in the lawns and around the mansions. Look for a superb fern-leaved beech (*Fagus sylvatica* 'Aspleniifolia') as well as sweet gums, a pin oak, an Indian bean tree, a tulip tree, chestnuts, gingko and both taxodium and metasequoia. However, I feel that the tree collection could have been better set out.

Another lake, known as the Potomac and popular for fishing, is hidden within a woodland copse. This was originally a clay pit and the water is deep. There is a folly on the bank, converted from the original pottery kiln. This is a peaceful, secluded part of the park, despite the nearby M4 and the Heathrow flight path overhead. The park is much used now, as very large areas have been provided for sports facilities, and golf and a putting green must help to recoup some of the cost of maintaining the site.

GUNNERSBURY TRIANGLE ECOLOGICAL PARK

W4

In an industrial and densely populated area is an unlikely little gem of defiant wilderness, a delightful interlude of only 6 acres sandwiched in a triangular plot of land between three railway lines. It was so inaccessible that it escaped development and since it was cut off from the world it has been an orchard, a source of sand and gravel, and allotments, before gradually returning to nature as birch and willow woodland.

However, in 1981 there was a threat of development for light industry, which spurred local action. A 'Save the Triangle' campaign was launched and the Chiswick Wildlife Group was formed. As a result, the value of the site as a conservation area was recognized and the Borough of Hounslow bought the site from British Rail with a grant from the Greater London Council. It was formally designated as a statutory Local Nature Reserve and it is one of the Trust's first reserves.

Light woodland dominates, but there are wet areas and depressions, possibly caused by digging out gravel. A nature trail leads the visitor around the perimeter areas and wheelchairs can follow the route, as there are ramps where necessary. The trail leads past a pond and marshland as well as wet woodland to an open meadow site. As you pass beside tangles of brambles, you see carpets of bluebells, followed by cow parsley, geraniums and anemones. The inevitable urban interloper willow herb has settled in with other wild flowers, beneath blossoming native trees and survivors from the orchard. There are flag irises and reeds around the pools and occasional seats for pausing to reflect. The experience of nature here is all the more remarkable because in places the paths encounter the railway line and tube trains rattle past.

Most of the plant life has regenerated naturally over the last forty or so years and there are now about 200 species of plants. Nearly fifty bird species have been recorded as well, including tawny owls, greater spotted woodpeckers, redpoll and warblers; their songs on summer days offset the rumble of the trains. Species of butterflies and other insects have increased as the ecological balance has restored itself – a great tribute to the carers. This is a community garden too, and there is a small portakabin that doubles as a reception area and is beautifully painted with a woodland scene of birds and foxgloves.

Right White villas on the crest of the hill at Gunnersbury, seen behind the spiralling trunk of a sweet chestnut tree.

PALACES AND PASTORAL PROSPECTS

HAMPTON COURT, TWICKENHAM, RICHMOND AND KEW

PALACES AND PASTORAL PROSPECTS
Hampton Court, Twickenham, Richmond and Kew

Royal Botanic Gardens, Kew, Marble Hill House, York House, Hampton Court Palace,
Bushy Park, Richmond Park, Ham House, Barnes Wildfowl and Wetlands Trust

The River Thames is the reason for London being where it is. Londinium was established on the spot where the Romans, arriving from France through Kent, could span the river with a bridge. But the river's silver thread also proved to offer the easiest passage through the Thames valley, much of which was densely forested. The journey by boat upstream made the banks of the river fifteen miles south-west of London a convenient and attractive site for a royal palace and Hampton Court Palace became the country home of the monarch from 1529, when Henry VIII acquired it from Cardinal Wolsey, until the accession of George III in 1760.

Hampton Court and other royal palaces, at Kew and Richmond, enticed the nobility and gentry to follow the royals, and throughout the seventeenth and eighteenth centuries they built their own grand houses along the river. One of these was Ham House, the home of the wealthy and powerful earls of Dysart. For the nobility, the proximity of Hampton Court Palace was a guarantee of status, and yet they still felt close to the city – location mattered as much then as it does today.

Away from the city, both royals and their followers sought the rude health attributed to rural living and revelled in rustic delights. Richmond Park served as a hunting forest for Richmond Palace and it was essential that the homes and palaces should have gardens. At Kew Palace Frederick, Prince of Wales, made a pleasure garden which grew to form the internationally famous Royal Botanic Gardens with its great plant collections The gardens of Ham House represent three centuries of distinguished gardening. Horace Walpole and Alexander Pope indulged in the eighteenth-century passion for gardens at the Countess of Suffolk's Marble Hill House. And the tradition of garden-making in this riverside area continued in the early twentieth century when an imposing Italianate garden was built at York House.

Richmond Palace is long gone, but today the park offers deer, wilderness and the famous sweeping view from Richmond Hill for the enjoyment of all. Fights in the past to secure public rights of access to the park reflect the urban dweller's awareness that well-being is maintained by the availability of countryside. Although very different from the estates of the monarchy and the gentry, the restored wetlands of Barnes have met this need too, with a wild environment that is surprisingly close to the heart of the city.

ROYAL BOTANIC GARDENS

KEW, SURREY

The length of the Royal Botanic Gardens at Kew, running almost north–south, follows the River Thames on one of its meanders. There is much to see and for those with only a day to spend a guidebook with a map is essential. Prioritizing is the key. The weather may simplify this and the many great glasshouses offer not only shelter but also huge rewards. The time of year will also help those bemused by choice, for the seasons suggest priorities, although there are evergreen areas, such as the bamboo garden, that are diverting at all times. Or it may be the huge old trees, the green vistas and the riverside that draw the visitor.

It all started in 1728 when Queen Caroline, consort to George II, rented Kew Palace as a country home for ninety-nine years for £100 and a fat deer. Their son Frederick, Prince of Wales, and his wife, Princess Augusta, lived next door, at Kew House. Frederick began making a pleasure garden and after his death Augusta created a small 'exotick' garden and arboretum.

Sir William Chambers, architect to the Princess, took on responsibility for the design; several temples, an orangery and a 'ruined' arch are largely his doing. The ten-storey Chinese pagoda also dates from his day. Few people realize that this was erected in 1761, it has stood the test of time so well. A dramatic 164-feet/50-metre-high focus, it once had gilded dragons on the roof.

With the accession of George III in 1760, the two estates were merged. Lancelot 'Capability' Brown was borrowed from his activities at nearby Richmond Lodge, another royal home, and the western side of Kew gardens, beside the Thames, is basically his work.

The botanist Sir Joseph Banks was asked to take over the running of the garden. He and William Aiton, the superintendent, with whom Banks enjoyed a forty-year collaboration, sent collectors around the world to acquire new and useful plants, and as a result Kew's botanic collection grew apace. Some plants seen in the gardens today, such as the bird of paradise plants, strelitzias, are thought to have grown from specimens of those rarities brought to Kew in the mid-eighteenth century. Banks sailed with Captain James Cook to the Pacific and many Australian plants, such as *Rosa banksiae*, acknowledge his name.

In 1840 the gardens were handed to the nation and Sir William Hooker, the rhododendron popularizer, took charge as the first official director. He was succeeded by his son Joseph. By this time it was crops and medicinal plants that were absorbing botanists and the expanding British Empire proved to offer a rewarding lucky dip. Quinine, a crucial medicine for malaria, became plentiful only after the seeds of Jesuit's bark (*Chinchona* spp.), brought to England from the Andes, became the source for thousands of trees distributed from Kew. Today, the Banks Building holds a collection of recognized useful plants from around the world.

The gardens expanded over the years as new plots were given by the royal family to the public: Queen Victoria donated Queen

---

Pages 164–165 This famous view from Richmond Hill shows the graceful meander of the River Thames as it flows past Ham House towards Teddington Lock.
Page 167 A side view of the restored Privy Garden at Hampton Court showing the terraces and carefully planned ornamental topiary.
Left On a summer evening the dark sky sets off the transparency of glass and water, dramatically highlighting the Palm House and the fountain of Hercules and the river god Achelous, at the Royal Botanic Gardens, Kew.

Page 170 Top: the extraordinary sculptural shapes of desert plants displayed in a section of the Princess of Wales Conservatory. Bottom left: plant families clearly ordered in the Herbaceous Ground. Bottom right: subtle textures in the ornamental grass beds.
Page 171 Top: the Syon Vista, an avenue walk, on a members' summer evening. Bottom left: vegetables and medicinal herbs growing in the Nosegay Garden. Bottom right: spiralling clipped holly amidst lavender in geometric parterres fronting Kew Palace.

Charlotte's Cottage and Edward VII gave Cambridge Cottage. The area now covers 300 acres of land: almost all of this is on the flood plain of the river, so the soil consists of deep layers of fine river gravels and sands, over London clay.

There is nowhere quite like Kew. Its history is such that it has accumulated very different areas of botanical expertise. It is old enough for collections of oak, ash, beech, birch, alder, willow, hollies and walnut to mature, with additions of exotic discoveries, such as tulip trees, gum trees, strawberry trees, the handkerchief tree and the Chilean monkey puzzles that so beguiled Victorians. Plants have not always been supplied by adventurous expeditions: some have been traded and some given – for example, the East India Company donated its collection soon after the Indian Mutiny.

The Rhododendron Dell, filled after Joseph Hooker's travels to the Himalayas, is a particularly popular area. It was dug out in the last quarter of the eighteenth century as part of the original plans by 'Capability' Brown. Today it has more hybrids than species. The azaleas are at their vibrant best in late May and June.

There are more acid beds in the Woodland Garden, where filtered light protects pretty trilliums and other North American ground cover plants such as *Cornus canadensis*, maianthemums and even little clintonias, followed later by the blue poppies of the Himalayas. This area, beside the Aeolus Mound, surmounted by a circular temple, is heady with the perfume of witch hazels in spring. And there are hellebores, hostas, lilies and primulas. Further away, near the Lion Gate, more acid lovers, the heathers, have two flowering periods, autumn then early spring.

A more remote, quieter area, north-west of the redwood glade, has yet a different atmosphere. Here the English countryside is celebrated in a nature reserve, with grasses and wild flowers. It is also well worth visiting the order beds, behind a high wall parallel with the Rock Garden, where, as in the old physic gardens, herbaceous perennials are shown in their family groups. It is fascinating to see the variety among them – take a look at the amazing umbellifers, for instance. The rectangular beds for ornamental grasses north-east of the Rock Garden are super from late July until the crispness of November, when the huge pampas plumes catch the low light of autumn.

The Rock Garden was laid out in 1882, inspired by an alpine valley. Between huge blocks of sandstone, there is a 'ravine' where a path wanders beneath a stone bridge. Many plants, including trailing conifers and tiny willows, cling to the contours of the rock, just as they would at high altitudes. Others, including saxifrages and small bulbs, take shelter in crevices.

There are over 50,000 species of plants at Kew, many of them under glass. The Temperate House, built by Decimus Burton in 1860, is among the largest greenhouses in the world, covering 48,000 square feet/4,500 square metres. The visitor moves from one geographical area to another. Here can be found the dragon tree (*Dracaena draco*) from the Canary Islands, which grows at a snail's pace – even in its homeland few can be seen. And there is possibly the world's largest greenhouse plant, *Jubaea chilensis*, a wine palm from Chile, raised from seed in 1846. Another plant, a cycad, *Encephalartos woodii*, from Natal, is possibly the last surviving specimen in the world. Some endangered species are propagated here for return to their homelands.

Adjacent is the Evolution House, a more recent construction of the 1950s. The fascination of geological time draws visitors past basic bacterial mud, swampy sulphur springs and coal forests, to emerge into our familiar green softness, feeling humbled, insignificant and relieved.

The visionary Palm House must be one of the most photographed buildings in the garden. This magnificent glasshouse (now guarded by a stony row of heraldic Queen's Beasts carved to celebrate the coronation of Elizabeth II) was built in 1848 as a co-operative project between the engineer Richard Turner and architect Decimus Burton. The engineering

Above Looking towards the mound and the Temple of Aeolus, over the summer display of the order beds near the rose pergola.

makes light of an arching metal-ribbed tunnel of glass, 360 feet/110 metres long and 62 feet/18 metres high. Its cast-iron structure includes high clerestory-like walkways, reached by spiralling steps. From these, visitors can peer over ornamental railings to look down upon a steamy green canopy of palms and bananas, and forests of fast-growing bamboo canes. A South African prickly cycad, *Encephalartos altensteinii*, sent to Kew in 1775, is the pride of the Palm House, being the oldest glasshouse plant in the world.

Next door is another masterpiece engineered by Richard Turner, the Water Lily House. Inside, exquisite lotus flowers from

Asia and Egypt are enhanced by finely foliaged papyrus alongside.

The newest glasshouse, the Princess of Wales Conservatory, has ten climatic zones, including a place for the giant water lilies *Victoria amazonica*. These have flat circular leaves of vast diameter, often 6½ feet/2 metres across, and are hugely popular. Grown each year from seed, they are strong enough to support the weight of small children, and allow them to float on the water surface.

There is colour and flower all year round. The winter-flowering cherries charm visitors in January and more blossom follows in February, when camellias add winter whites, ice-cream pinks and cardinal reds. Soon afterwards the Rock Garden begins its season of colour, adding more of the whites and pinks, plus blues and yellows. The warmth of spring colour starts in March and April with carpets of crocus, daffodils, tulips and bluebells. Herbaceous beds and annual bedding are summer joys and in autumn the foliage of maples and azaleas, with fruiting trees and shrubs, flares into warmth. All year the lake attracts birds, many acquired as ornamental specimens. They include black swans, mandarin ducks and even pelicans.

There is much else in this wonderful garden, from historical parterres and the Nosegay Garden to gazebos and the exotic plant portraits of the Marianne North Gallery. There is a Japanese gateway, from the Japan Exhibition of 1911, with a haiku carved in stone and lanterns along the paths. There are many fine buildings, such as the red-brick Dutch-style merchant house and the thatched picnic lodge known as Queen Charlotte's Cottage. Kew is above all famed for its worldwide identification of plant material, for conservation and for its educational role. It has charity status, supplemented by government grants.

Left The elegantly Palladian Marble Hill House seen across the cricket ground.

MARBLE HILL HOUSE
TWICKENHAM, MIDDLESEX

Both Marble Hill House and York House are in Twickenham, within visiting distance of Hampton Court Palace and Ham House, and close to another famed house, Horace Walpole's 'Little Gothic Castle' at Strawberry Hill.

Walpole was a friend of the Lady Henrietta Howard, late in her life when she was Countess of Suffolk. As a former mistress of George II when he was Prince of Wales, she had played a role at court, and after George's accession to the throne, he honoured her part in his life by giving her sufficient funds to build her own house. This she did beside the River Thames, creating Marble Hill, a compact, impeccably Palladian mansion with a magnificent view of the river. It is eternally preserved in a romantic landscape, *The Thames near Marble Hill*, painted in 1762 by Richard Wilson.

This area of London became the fashionable haunt for the 'glitterati' of the Age of Reason and among Henrietta's local friends was the poet, philosopher and landscaper Alexander Pope. He had leased a house along the river, where he made a famous garden. Pope's grotto, 'finished with shells interspersed with pieces of looking glass in angular forms', still exists today, now a mutilated shadow of its former glory, in the grounds of a convent school. He and Charles Bridgeman, landscaper to the King, planned Marble Hill garden together, with the lady of the house taking an active part.

The central view of the river was the essence of the garden, protected on either side by rectangular groves of fine chestnut trees. There were garden buildings, of which today only an icehouse and a rather gloomy grotto remain. Nevertheless, the sweeping lawns and trees still have much charm and it is worth finding the truly majestic black walnut tree, *Juglans nigra*, that survives from Lady Henrietta's day.

YORK HOUSE
TWICKENHAM, MIDDLESEX

The garden of York House overlays ancient grazing meadows. The garden, divided by a riverside road, partly runs along the river. Visitors may approach through a contemporary sculpture garden at Champions Wharf gate and follow the attractive terraced riverside walk, after which the garden comes as an unexpected revelation. Italianate and formal, it has an amazingly over-scaled fountain that would be more at home in the blazing heat of the Palace of Caserta, near Naples, than beside the misty Thames.

The imagination and opulent style of the garden are those of the former owner, an Indian merchant prince, Sir Ratan Tata, who bought the late-seventeenth-century mansion in 1906 and laid out the gardens. It was he who created the fountain, an elaborate amassing of rocks on which are draped larger-than-life marble nymphs, who claw their way up huge boulders or lounge in adoring fashion at the feet of a goddess driving a winged horse. Water pours from massive conch shells to a pool below, in which water lilies float and flag irises and ferns provide dense cover, from which the water-nymphs emerge. The costly marbles were transported from Italy to be sited as the theatrical focus for the rest of the formal Italianate layout. Yew hedges clinch the symmetry and there is another small, perfectly circular, pool at the far end, in balance but unchallenging.

An elegant stone footbridge strides the road, connecting the riverside garden to the house where there is an open sunken lawn, ideal for summer performances of Shakespeare plays. Beside it is a more secluded area with a distinctly Victorian feel, overlaid by local authority practicality. Richmond Borough Council, who bought the property in 1923, is working towards restoring this unlikely treasure.

Left One Italian marble nymph hauling another up from the depths of the pond at York House.

HAMPTON COURT PALACE

HAMPTON, SURREY

In 1514, the year before he became Cardinal and Lord Chancellor of England, Thomas Wolsey acquired from the Knights Hospitallers of St John a large estate on the banks of the Thames fifteen miles south-west of London and easily reached by barge. Here he built himself a magnificent palace and established the first of the great gardens of England. When he fell from favour, he 'gave' the whole property to Henry VIII, hoping to be reinstated, but to no avail. In 1529 he was banished, his lands declared forfeit, and Henry moved in. The whole site was enclosed to provide royal hunting land. Five of Henry's six wives lived at the palace for various periods and his only son, Edward VI, spent most of his short life there.

Henry was keen on gardens and as soon as he acquired Hampton Court he set about its garden with a passion. The gardens by the river were adorned with the 'Kinges bestes': golden heraldic emblems of 'lyon', dragon, horse, greyhound and others, each mounted upon a white and green post. The influence of such Tudor ornamentation can be seen today in, for instance, stone beasts at Kew and modern clipped ones at Hall Place (see page 226). Formal geometric patterns dominated the layout and the heraldic figures were dotted extravagantly around these sites.

Successive monarchs all left their mark at the Hampton Court gardens. Elizabeth I actually gardened 'briskly when alone', but, mindful of her image, she 'went slowly and marched with leisure' when observed. In Elizabethan times, flower gardens were often divided into four sections, influenced by the pattern of Moorish gardens seen by travelling crusaders. The adventurers Sir Walter Ralegh, Sir John Hawkins and Sir Francis Drake all

Right A magical long vista into Hampton Court park, viewed through handsome gates from the semi-circular canal in the grounds of the palace.

brought back exotics from their travels, including tobacco and the potato, and these were grown with care in the hothouses at Hampton Court. James I, although he was more inclined to hunt than garden, appointed Inigo Jones to manage the estate. Charles I redesigned the gardens again, making new ponds, basins and fountains plus an eleven-mile channel bringing water to feed them (see page 183). After the Restoration, Charles II also had a go at remodelling, working mostly on the Home Park – the large area of grazing parkland cut through by the Long Water and now the site for the annual Royal Horticultural Society flower show. He had picked up ideas during his exile in France and Holland. He made a huge semi-circular lawn with radiating avenues focused upon the palace, a *patte d'oie* or goosefoot design, with the Long Water as the central axis.

William and Mary, coming from Holland, were even more influenced by the geometric patterns fashionable there, adding decorative evergreens as ornaments and boundaries. They also developed the Great Fountain Garden that was central to the semi-circular garden of Charles II's scheme, adding more waterworks and filling the grassed spaces with scrolled patterns of dwarf box hedging set in gravel and ornamented with coloured sand.

It is presumed that it was the decision of William and Mary to create the Wilderness where once there had been an orchard. This too had a geometric design, in which 'rooms' were separated by straight paths. But mostly William is remembered for the Privy Garden, because of its fancy Baroque styling with parterres, cutwork and a seventeenth-century planting scheme of flowers such as hollyhocks, violas, larkspur, irises and roses.

Left Hampton Court Palace and the famous inverted-cone-shaped yews, viewed in the early morning from a showground pontoon bridge that temporarily crosses the Long Water.
Right Looking back towards the palace through the recently restored pergola tunnel alongside the Privy Garden.

Dating from 1702, the design, based upon *gazon coupé* or patterned turf, was elaborated further by clipped sculptured yews and fine box edging. The Privy Garden occupies the land between the palace and the river, once reserved for the royal family only.

The next monarch, Queen Anne, had to pay off her predecessors' garden-making debts, and was perhaps disinclined to amass more of her own. The hornbeam maze, however, was probably made for her. Georges I and II added little to the gardens.

George III gave 'Capability' Brown residence at Hampton Court under the title of Master Gardener. While living here Brown planned the landscapes of Richmond Palace and some of Kew but he left the formality of Hampton Court undisturbed. One of the things he did was, in 1769, to plant the Great Vine, still alive today and thriving, its 'Black Hamburg' grapes being duly collected every September. William IV carried out some renovation and Queen Victoria opened the park and gardens to the public, a move that ultimately led to a change of ownership. Now the grounds of the palace are part of the Crown Estates, managed by the Historic Palaces Trust.

Today there is much to see in the 66 acres of garden, and on any one visit it may be worth selecting what is of interest rather than undertaking an exhaustive race around the whole garden. For flower enthusiasts there are the much-admired herbaceous beds planted in the early twentieth century. The Wilderness is now a place for named trees and massed daffodils in spring, and the ancient Maze will entertain those who come with children. But for me it is the grand scale and vistas of the Great Fountain Garden, with its expansive fan-shaped layout, that haunts the memory.

The recent restoration of the Privy Garden invites the visitor to take a fascinating step back in time. At the far end are the Tijou screens, wrought-iron gilded gates made by Jean Tijou in the early eighteenth century and intended for the Great Fountain Garden but now beside the River Thames. The old Pond Garden, or Sunken Garden, is the place to see brilliant bedding plants. There is a walk around the garden, where 'windows' in the surrounding hedge frame views of the plants. Closely associated is a compact knot garden of 1924, designed with Tudor flourish. Over 100,000 bedding plants are grown in the glasshouses, many being propagated by cuttings for continuity in the summer displays.

The RHS Flower Show

Every July the Royal Horticultural Society holds a major flower show at Hampton Court Palace. One of the largest flower shows in the world, it is very different from the Chelsea Flower Show (see page 97). The site is more spacious. It is also held later in the season, so the flowers are those of mid- to late summer rather than spring to early summer. The displays are nearly all south of the Long Water and if you park on the north side you reach them by crossing one of three pontoon bridges, a not-to-be-missed opportunity to see the palace from the centre of the Long Water. An alternative way of arriving at Hampton Court is to float slowly upriver to the palace from London.

New products, new techniques and stylish garden ornaments are on display. There are many show gardens, large and small, including a separate section of water gardens on the north side of the Long Water. The central pavilion, sponsored by the *Daily Mail*, always has a spectacular large garden. For some visitors the British Rose Festival marquee is the main draw but others may prefer the floral display tents. Here specialist nurseries show new hybrids as well as old favourites, and plants can be bought and stored in a crèche, leaving the

Opposite Delighted children had a major role in creating a special vegetable and compost garden for the RHS Hampton Court Flower Show.

visitor free to explore the site. Enthusiasts with specialist interests will find experts available to discuss horticultural problems. Others may be more interested in selections from the national plant collections, put on by the National Council for the Conservation of Plants and Gardens.

BUSHY PARK
HAMPTON, SURREY

Bushy Park was once part of the Hampton Court Estate, the two together making up a huge estate of over 2,000 acres. A wide, mile-long avenue of ranked horse chestnut trees slices through

the park, leading directly to Hampton Court Palace. Sir Christopher Wren originally planned it, on the orders of William III, as part of a grand northern approach to the palace that included a superbly proportioned circular pool, concentrically ringed by a wide expanse of lawn and drive; a lime tree avenue radiates westwards. In the centre of the pool is a bronze statue of Diana the huntress, moved here in 1713 from the Privy Garden of the palace. This and the magnificent double line of horse chestnuts on either side of the ride establish the central formal axis of the park. The undersides of

the trees are levelled by browsing deer, giving all the silhouettes of the chestnuts a horizontal base with light on the green grass sweeping through beneath, magically characteristic of much English parkland. The trees are covered by white 'candle' flowers in late spring – once a popular time when, on the day known as Chestnut Sunday, people drove from London just to see the avenue. Elsewhere the greensward of the park is

Above Centrally placed in the circular pool, the fountain of Diana lies on the mile-long axis of the wide chestnut avenue, originally planned by Wren as the grand northern approach to Hampton Court Palace.

studded with single trees and plantations of oaks and limes.

Fallow and red deer wander at will among the stately lines of trees as well as within the copses and the wilder reaches of the park. But, because they could damage the tree and shrub collection, they are kept out of the beautiful Waterhouse Woodland Gardens in the western part of the estate. Here is a hidden unexpected pleasure, an intimate glade within closely meshed trees, with some specials such as Persian ironwood

Above Wonderful Bushy Park, where light and deer creep beneath the avenues of chestnut trees.

(*Parrotia persica*) and dawn redwood (*Metasequoia glyptostroboides*). The flowering shrubs include rhododendrons and camellias. Near by is a tumbling waterfall, part of the Longford River, which suits the animated character of this area. The spirit here is quite different from the rest of the park, which is quietly tranquil, both in the wilderness and the spacious open formality of the main parkland.

It is in the west of the park that the Longford River, sourced from the River Colne, begins its controlled journey, as devised by Charles I, to supply Hampton Court Palace with water for

RICHMOND PARK
RICHMOND, SURREY

Like Alexandra Palace in north London and Greenwich Park in south-east London, Richmond Park offers magnificent views of the spreading metropolis below. Rumour has it that the Henry VIII mound, a prehistoric hillock, was the site where Henry watched for signalled confirmation of the death of Anne Boleyn.

Richmond was the site of the palace of Shene, where Edward III lived, followed by Richard II, who, having expanded the building, later burned most of it down in his grief at the death by plague of his wife, Anne. Later, Henrys V, VI and VII all resided here, but the palace was destroyed by fire in 1499. Henry VII rebuilt it, and in token of this it took its name from his title of Earl of Richmond in Yorkshire. Elizabeth spent less time there, but the Earl of Leicester, Lord Cecil, Sir Francis Walsingham, Sir Walter Ralegh and Sir Philip Sydney all lived near by.

In 1625, when Charles I moved to Richmond Palace to avoid plague, he enclosed the land with a brick wall to contain the hunting. However, sensible of local fury, he continued to allow public access to the old tracks and bridleways, adding six gated entrances, all still in use. Roads cross the park, allowing cars through. But the roads are mostly around the perimeter and the only way really to immerse yourself in the park is on foot.

In 1649, at the time of the Commonwealth, Parliament passed an Act giving Richmond Great Park to the City of London, a gesture towards the idea of parks for the people which – although the land was later returned to Charles II – laid the foundation for the park's public use.

Much of the character of the parkland depends upon the grazing herds of deer that roam freely around the 2,500 acres of the park, guarded and culled by gamekeepers and still providing

the fountains. The watercourse was carefully engineered to flow through a culvert under the road to feed the Long Water and canals of Hampton Court. But the small stream also follows a course to the east, sometimes in small straight channels, sometimes meandering, to open out into the Heron Pond and eventually the Leg of Mutton Pond on the eastern side of the avenue. The gentle stream appears quite natural, fitting in with both the formality, the 'pleasance' of the area's design and the wilderness of the parkland. Ducks, geese and herons are contented here in the shallow, quietly moving water.

Although roads allow cars through the park, they are not intrusive and barely feature in much of the parkland. Indeed the western area seems quite remote, almost like natural countryside. Here wild grasses and native plants provide cover for about fifty species of birds and many of the smaller wild animals. Bushy Park now covers over 1,100 acres, much frequented since Queen Victoria opened it to the public in 1838.

Above In one of the wilder parts of Richmond Park, a log gently steams in the early morning sun.

venison for royal and other tables. The tall red deer are native but the little spotted fallow deer were brought to England by the Normans. In the rutting season the deer's eerie calls echo through the autumn mist. But deer are far from the only wildlife. As they emerge from bracken foxes slink away, badgers dig in, owls hoot from the woods, water birds congregate at the ponds and rabbits race to ground.

Above Dew shines on the grass beneath a tree near the Pen Ponds in early autumn.

The park has several interesting buildings. Pembroke Lodge, perched above the river with a fine view towards Windsor Castle, was enlarged in 1788 by Sir John Soane and was the childhood home of the philosopher Bertrand Russell. Now there is a café and terraced gardens for formal display of roses and summer bedding, a great contrast with the wilderness behind. Princess Alexandra lives in the eighteenth-century Thatched House Lodge, once the home of Sir Robert Walpole, the first prime minister. White Lodge, right in the middle, is a Palladian mansion built in 1727 as a hunting lodge for George II, and it has welcomed many distinguished figures, including Lord Nelson, William Pitt and Walter Scott. Edward VIII was born there. It is now the home of the Royal Ballet School.

The classic parkland landscape of Richmond Park runs along the Thames, high on the natural terrace, mostly spacious grassland with spreads of bracken. Most of the trees are oak and many are very old, spreading widely but trimmed from beneath by deer. There are many wooded plantations, initially planted in the early nineteenth century with native trees, providing timber and cover for shooting. The main ones are Spanker's Hill and Sidmouth Wood. The undergrowth of rhododendrons was planted in Victorian times as cover for pheasants. A little later, the Isabella Plantation was created, where oak, beech and sweet chestnuts hold sway above camellias and azaleas. In the park there are streams and pools filled by water pumped from the two Pen Ponds which were made in the mid-eighteenth century to provide fishing as an alternative to the game. They are wonderfully unfussy, with plain grass surrounds and stocked with bream, carp, pike and perch. During the Second World War the Pen Ponds were drained because they made an obvious landmark for enemy aircraft.

Other popular needs are met by cricket pitches, golf courses and numerous football fields, as well as some of the wildest walking in London, all within the 13-mile perimeter. Meanders of the Thames can be seen glittering in reflected skylight and the distant horizon seems very far away. Even today, the broad sweep of the landscape could almost be the fine prospect of the eighteenth century. It is remarkable that this huge wild place is situated and protected within greater London.

The song 'Sweet Lass of Richmond Hill' refers to the bosky rise, where many a grand house was built in the eighteenth century, overlooking the panorama of the Thames Valley. Today it is crowned by the Star and Garter Home, once an inn with smart assembly rooms and now a home for disabled soldiers.

Isabella Plantation

The source of the name is unclear. An early map refers to 'Isabell slade' meaning yellow valley. Today it is a steep wooded garden of roughly 42 acres, a surprise garden hidden by trees within the wilderness of Richmond Park, but revealed every spring by the thousands of visitors trekking down the hill and plunging into the indigenous woodland. There they find an amazing sight of pastel and hotly coloured azaleas in the company of tall rhododendrons, exotic magnolias, fragrant witch hazels and glossy camellias, with consolidated mats of heather, all revelling in the acid soils and dappled shade. Here is the national collection of Kurume azaleas, many brought back from the Far East by E.H. Wilson early in the twentieth century. In April and May, the best way is to enter from the south. Once inside the gate, turn left and follow the tiny 'ravine' down beside thick cumulus mounds of dwarf azaleas, sometimes crossing small footbridges, and you will eventually move out from the dark canopy into sunny glades where different plants thrive.

At other times of the year this wonderful woodland garden is cooler in hue and gentler in feeling. In spring waterside plants along the streams and in the bogs include butter-yellow kingcups, flowering reeds and flag iris. There are spreads of daffodils, primroses and bluebells set among ferns. In summer Japanese iris, day lilies and candelabra primulas bring quieter colour, together with foxgloves in the shadows among the woodrush. In autumn the many different Japanese acers bring strong colour again, adding to the russet foliage of beech.

The plantation, like the sanctuary at Sidmouth Wood, also in the park, is a haven for birds, being home to many species including tree creepers, yellowhammers, great tits, pheasants,

Opposite Fragrant azaleas flash their brilliant colours on either side of the tiny ravine that runs downhill through the Isabella Plantation.

woodpeckers and jackdaws. All seem well pleased to spend time among the flowering shrubs and tall trees. Thompson's Pond, in a green grassed glade in the park, attracts herons, mallards, mandarin ducks and Canada geese. Among the native trees are some rare ones including Tibetan cherry, Himalayan birch, snake bark maple, tupelo (*Nyssa sylvatica*) and Japanese snowbell (*Styrax japonicus*).

HAM HOUSE
HAM, SURREY

Jacobean Ham House, built in 1610, was embellished sixty years later by the Countess of Dysart and her second husband, the 1st Duke of Lauderdale. Between them they created the palatial mansion that it is still, now under the care of the National Trust, which has lovingly restored its seventeenth-century detail.

The situation could not have been bettered. John Evelyn visited in 1678 and described the various wonders of the garden 'and all this at the banks of the Sweetest River in the World'. The house faces the River Thames, with spacious grounds to the rear and a formally enclosed forecourt, covering about twenty acres in all. In the forecourt there are thirty-eight portrait busts, including representations of Charles I and II, as well as Roman emperors and other antique figures, all set into oval niches in the walls around a circular lawn with a large Coade stone river god reclining on a rock as its centrepiece. Evergreen topiary of box, laurel and bay is set around the garden in balanced symmetry.

The Lauderdales' gardens were as glamorous as the house. From the beginning they were geometric and orderly, with superbly formal displays that required ingenious setting out and equally thoughtful aftercare. Plans and notes at the time make it clear that nothing was left to chance. A drawing of about 1672 shows the design by John Slezer and Jan Wyck on which the National Trust has based its restoration. The plain terrace can be seen setting the house above the gardens and opening up a view to Richmond Hill, through a railed *clairvoyée* in the brick wall. Ornamenting the area were pineapples made of Coade stone. Below the terrace, the South Garden is laid in a simple rectangular grid of lawns, known as plats. Each probably had a central sculpture, very likely cast in lead. There would have been many painted wooden boxes containing orange and lemon trees, myrtles, oleanders and pomegranates, moved indoors to the orangery in winter. These are now appearing again under the ownership of the Trust. At one time 327 pots were listed, also gradually being restored to the site.

In the distance is the late seventeenth-century Wilderness, one of the few originals left in the country. Far from being wild, the Wilderness too is orderly, with radiating paths, lined on either side by hornbeam hedges, leading from a central circle to a round painted summerhouse topped with a golden ball. All areas were set with sculptures and with seats and wooden boxes planted for summer fragrance. Each interior space had an entrance and these 'doors' led into 'rooms', now a familiar concept but then unusual and romantic. Each segment was planted with shrubs, field maples and hawthorns or rough-cut grasses with wild flowers; this was as naturalistic as the garden ever got.

Subsequent owners on the whole resisted the fashionable eighteenth-century romantic 'naturalness' of 'Capability' Brown, restricting themselves to replacing some seventeenth-century parterres on the south front with clumps of trees and shrubs. The Cherry Garden, to the east of the house, is a strikingly beautiful restoration. Don't expect a cherry orchard – the cherries were probably confined to the house walls. Instead wander along the tunnels of hornbeam *à berceaux* (that is, in the form of vaulted trellis) and look through *clairvoyées* across the

Above Once a watering pond for animals, the pond at Ham Common is now maintained as a habitat for wildlife.

open space, which is divided into triangular sections by diagonal gravelled paths lined with immaculately clipped box. The spaces of this simple knot garden are filled with Dutch lavender and dwarf grey santolina. Both are clipped into a matrix of dome shapes in early spring, filling the beds with soft

Above Restored thirty years ago to the style of the late seventeenth century, the Cherry Garden of Ham House is patterned with alternating grey-leaved lavender and santolina, enclosed by a hornbeam tunnel.

grey mounds; later the santolina is clipped again but the lavender is allowed to flower, creating a lovely contrast of texture and colour. At every corner a sharply clipped cone of box prevents the garden from being too sentimental.

The gardens have been beautifully and subtly restored and work is still in progress. The walled garden beside the Orangery is mostly grassed, but it will be returned to the original grid layout of the past, in which large rectangular beds were planted

to supply food for the house. Already two beds have been planted and the colours, textures and scents sustain the visitor who pauses for bodily refreshment at the Orangery restaurant – a rest will be welcome, because visiting the house and garden will easily occupy a whole day. By late summer the new beds are vibrantly coloured with ornamental vegetables such as yellow and red-stemmed Swiss chard, red orach, peppers, pumpkins and gourds. Huge artichokes add luminous lilac flowers; pretty orange-flowering runner beans climb up poles alongside hops and light-blue flowering morning glory. All are melded together with the scarlets, oranges and yellows of nasturtiums and marigolds and cobalt blue cornflowers. Scented and culinary herbs fill in, adding to the exotic perfume of citrus trees in tubs.

Appropriately, more exotica is available close to the garden at the Palm Centre, a nursery in Ham, where citrus trees as well as date palms, feather palms, fan palms, bamboos and massive tree ferns are on sale or to be seen.

BARNES WILDFOWL AND WETLANDS TRUST

SW13

A recent unique partnership between the Wildfowl and Wetlands Trust, Thames Water and Berkeley Homes has made possible the most beautiful wild reserve in London. The co-operative scheme that the partners worked out has received international acclaim and its success indicates a way forward for similar public ventures.

At Barnes the winding course of the lower Thames sweeps around old Victorian reservoirs and land that was once ancient farmland and market gardens founded on the silt of former

Left The calm after the storm; a rainbow arches over the beautiful wetlands at Barnes.

marshes. After an improvement scheme in 1980, which means that water is now provided from the non-tidal Thames directly to the reservoirs of the Lea Valley, the reservoirs were no longer needed. The area was already attracting wildlife and had been declared a Site of Special Scientific Interest in 1975, so the vast space could not be used for mass housing. Instead, under the inspiration of Sir Peter Scott's wetlands at Slimbridge on the shores of the Severn Estuary, the idea was born of creating wetlands here – uniquely, in an urban area.

Work began in 1995. Recycling was a major part of the commitment, so the mass of concrete around the old reservoirs was crushed to make dry paths, strengthen shorelines and create a deep water reef as a nursery for fish. The soils were sorted and remixed to make six basic groups (during this process one area was found to contain an unexploded bomb). Ultimately, over thirty different wetland habitats were made, involving the planting of almost 30,000 trees and shrubs and huge numbers of aquatic plants. Boardwalks were constructed,

inviting the public into the heart of the bogs and pools, and hides were built for quiet observation. The Peter Scott Visitors' Centre is a glassed observatory, which has been likened to an airport terminal for birds. Here refreshment is available at a waterside café, and there are film shows, a discovery centre, a gallery, interactive touch screens, lectures and, of course, the *raison d'être* of the site, a place for watching birds on and over the deep lake where ducks, herons and cormorants feast upon fish.

A guidebook describes walks through the World's Wetlands, artificially built habitats that can be explored as a safari, where the visitor passes first from Arctic tundra, through the northern forests of Scandinavia, Siberia and the Canadian Shield. Then you may visit a Middle Eastern reed bed, cross the flood plains of Africa and South America, explore a tropical swamp forest, tour Asian rice fields, see an Australian billabong and experience oceanic islands as different as Hawaii and the Falklands. This tour of the world is completed by New Zealand, a country that could itself be a world national park. Rare ducks, geese and swans are settled in each special habitat.

For a totally different experience, follow the other walk, the Wildside, where the ponds, lakes and lagoons provide native habitats with indigenous trees and plants. Here the reservoir lagoon is deep with artificial reefs for fish, attracting divers such as ducks and cormorants. The reed beds provide a sanctuary for reed buntings and sedge warblers. Shallow mud suits herons, dabbling ducks and widgeon. And the main lake and sheltered lagoon host wintering birds including pochard, gadwall, shoveler and tufted ducks, and provide reedy shoreline for summer nesting birds such as ducks, grebes and kingfishers. Migrating birds like lapwings and redshanks stop over in winter.

Altogether the centre attracts over 140 different bird species, some of them rarely seen in London, like goshawk, curlew,

Above Thick reed beds surround a clear pool at Barnes wetlands.

sandpiper and cattle egret. From the tallest of the specially designed hides, where visitors can watch the birds without disturbing them, you can see an extensive 360° panorama of the reserve surrounded by the city profile. This hide, known as the Peacock Tower, has a lift for disabled visitors, and inside are benches and slit windows, plus informative paintings showing the seasonal changes of landscape and birdlife. A two-storey hide in the Wildside has views of the reservoir lagoon and grazing marsh. Many of the hides have sustainable living roof coverings of stonecrop and turf.

Native willows dominate the site, with waterside rushes including the tall swaying common reed (*Phragmites australis*), brown flowers of reed mace (*Typha latifolia*), common bull-rush (*Schoenoplectus lacustris*), the compact small rush (*Typha minima*) and the pretty flowering rush (*Butomus umbellatus*). These, with sedges and grasses, merge with other marginals such as yellow flag irises (*Iris pseudacorus*) and North American sweet flags (*Acorus calamus*). Colour comes from plants such as kingcups, primulas, purple and yellow loosestrife, pink flowering water plantago, creamy spirea and blue myosotis. Water lilies and azolla float on the water surface, with blanket weed and water horsetail (*Equisetum fluviatile*). All are plotting take-overs and must be restrained.

The wetlands look wonderfully natural but they are carefully managed to prevent the whole area from reverting to impassable jungle with invasive plants ruling turgid dirty water. Constant vigilance and maintenance are necessary, even though the reed beds do a great job of cleaning the water, for otherwise the open stretches of water would rapidly close over, and tranquillity turn into turmoil. Just as with painting the Forth Bridge, work can never cease. Invaluable assistance is offered by volunteer helpers such as the retired professional who told me how he looked forward to his one day a week working outdoors.

The wetlands are a celebration not only of water but also of light. In this open airy space – a rare thing in a city – you can see the light of the sky changing by the hour as well as the season. The many lakes and pools reflect the sky, increasing the sense of timeless space. And it is from the sky that the birds come to settle in the wetlands that offer them food and security. Some areas are sheltered and quiet, kept for breeding and roosting; others are alive with noisy exchanges.

Conservation is important here and the breeding programme is serious: for example, water voles have recently been released here in the hope that they may settle and multiply.

Three garden designers have created gardens based upon contemporary ideals, without lawn, peat or use of pesticides, herbicides or fertilizers. The ideas are provocative, challenging visitors to rethink their idea of what a garden is. One, by Land Art, Isabelle van Groeningen and Gabriella Pape, uses slate to create a spiralling path with massed perennials and grasses chosen to attract insects and other wildlife. Another, by Cleve West and Johnny Woodford, makes a witty connection between Barnes and Barnes Wallis of 'bouncing bomb' fame in the Second World War: a sculpture bounces across a long pool, skimming the water surface. All the materials are recycled and water conservation is the theme. Spare planting of drought-resistant plants contrasts with a lush reed bed filter. A third garden, by Arne Maynard, makes flowing walls of split oak logs topped with turf, much of which will eventually rot down to create habitats for hibernating amphibians beneath the semi-shade of silver birches.

These wetlands are probably the most surprising of all the gardens described in this book. They acknowledge the new-millennium concerns for nature: here an environment has been created where work can be done on the scientific understanding of ecological balance and conservation as well as the value of biodiversity. The place is also extremely beautiful.

RENOVATION AND INNOVATION
Lambeth, Southwark and Greenwich

*Museum of Garden History, Bonnington Square, Roots and Shoots, Brockwell Park,
Burgess Park and Chumleigh Multicultural Gardens, Greenwich Park*

Like all old cities, London has undergone many changes. Greenwich Palace once boasted what was the grandest of English parks, which reached its apogee in the time of the Stuarts. However, like all the royal palaces, Greenwich suffered from the fluctuations of royal enthusiasm, and after the reign of Charles II the park was neglected. The fine prospect from the green hill is a constant, though. Fully opened to the public in Victorian times, although still classified as a royal park, Greenwich Park will always be a highlight of this area, where visitors can enjoy both the sweeping parkland and the rich history of its surrounding buildings.

On a smaller but nevertheless substantial scale, another green and hilly park opened to the public in Victorian times, Brockwell Park, provides welcome respite from its built-up surroundings in Brixton.

Change continues to be the name of the game along the south bank of the river. Much came about as a result of the upheavals of war. During the Second World War Lord Abercrombie's Greater London Plan recognized that the devastation wrought by bombing in Southwark could be turned to advantage and a large new park could be built, providing green space where it was most needed in this densely populated area. Burgess Park, still to be finished, an adventurous enterprise where the different communities have a major impact, is the result.

The vision and hard work of individuals has brought other parks and gardens to this area. Not too far away from Burgess Park, are two other community gardens. One is at Bonnington Square, growing on what was once derelict bomb-scarred land; the other is Roots and Shoots, where industrial wasteland is now a flowery paradise. The commitment and energy of local residents, who protected the sites and raised funds for them, have enabled beauty and greenery to emerge from scenes of desolation.

The charming Museum of Garden History also has a history of rescue, for its success is thanks to a few people who recognized the value of the small church of St Mary-at-Lambeth and its burial ground. Plants thrive here, as they do at the community gardens, tended by volunteers and maintained by grants and charity. In this case, as at Greenwich Park, its history – in terms both of its location beside Lambeth Palace and of the contents it displays – adds to its appeal.

MUSEUM OF GARDEN HISTORY
SE1

Next to Lambeth Palace on the south bank of the Thames, where the archbishops of Canterbury have resided since 1200, is the church of St Mary-at-Lambeth. At the time of the Silver Jubilee of Elizabeth II in 1977, St Mary's church was derelict. But thanks to the persistence of some brave supporters, the church was saved from demolition and given Grade II listing, and a public appeal was launched for funds to create a museum of garden history. Generous donations were received and the Department of the Environment matched the sum raised, enabling the building to be repaired and fitted out as a museum, with space for exhibitions, lectures and concerts.

In the small burial ground beside the church, a replica of a seventeenth-century knot garden was created, designed by the Marchioness of Salisbury of Hatfield House. Opened by the Queen in 1983, it is planted with trees, shrubs and flowers associated with the seventeenth century and the Tradescant family. A huge old brick wall marking the boundary between the palace and the church grounds makes a splendid backdrop for climbing plants and an old mulberry tree.

The John Tradescants, father and son, were famous gardeners and plant collectors. They were gardeners to two kings, Charles I and II. The elder travelled to Russia, Algiers, the Low Countries and France, bringing to England many of our familiar garden plants. As his status grew he acquired a fine house in Lambeth with land attached so that he could propagate plants from his travels. He was appointed Keeper of the Botanic Garden in Oxford, but died before moving there.

His son travelled even further, his journeys including several visits to Virginia. He followed his father in his obsessive cataloguing of plants, eventually producing the *Musaeum Tradescantianum*, published in 1656. After his death, a colleague, Elias Ashmole, founded the Ashmolean Museum at Oxford in 1683, based upon the Tradescants' 'Collection of Rareties'.

Both Tradescants are buried in the grounds of St Mary's Church, along with Elias Ashmole, six archbishops and Captain Bligh of *Bounty* fame. And around their graves the garden flourishes. The knot of box hedges contains plants known in the seventeenth century, including foxgloves, lychnis, irises, poppies, spotted hawkweed, geraniums, santolina, calendula, black mustard, acanthus, martagon lilies, feverfew, rosemary, dictamnus, Solomon's seal, *Plantago major* 'Atrorubens' and of course tradescantias. By mid-summer these plants almost smother the box with a fragrant abundance of colours and textures. There are some old roses too, such as the Jacobite rose (*Rosa × alba* 'Maxima'), the musk rose (*Rosa moschata*) and striped *Rosa gallica* 'Versicolor', known also as Rosa Mundi. A spiralling holly (*Ilex × altaclerensis* 'Golden King') provides a central focus, with two large strawberry trees (*Arbutus unedo*) and red-barked *Arbutus × andrachnoides*, sequential in fruit and flower, overlooking the lot. The garden is a beautiful and gentle place for quiet reflection, albeit beside racetrack roads.

The museum is small and very welcoming. It has the largest collection of garden implements in the UK and owns John Evelyn's copy of *Musaeum Tradescantianum*. Garden and plant history lectures held here are popular during winter and the museum has a fast-growing membership of Friends, many of whom are also volunteers who maintain the lovely garden.

Pages 194–195 At night the beautifully lit linear landscape of trees beside Tate Modern, designed by Dieter Kienast, focuses attention upon the dome of St Paul's across the river.
Page 197 On the south bank of the river, the setting sun illuminates the delicate profile of the London Eye's huge wheel.
Left The knot garden at the Museum of Garden History encloses plants known in England in the seventeenth century; in the centre is a spiral of variegated holly, and a banana tree grows by the wall of Lambeth Palace.

BONNINGTON SQUARE
SW8

This site, bomb-damaged in the Second World War, remained curiously unnoticed, its potential unrecognized, until 1990. Awakened to its potential, residents formed the Bonnington Square Garden Association, which put a proposal to the council to save the area for the well-being of local people. They were successful and a government grant and sponsorship were awarded to make a garden.

Bonnington Square is truly a pleasure garden, or, in the words of the initial proposal, a 'Paradise Project'. The two horticulturists who were involved in its creation, English Dan Pearson and James Fraser, a New Zealander, have combined tranquil English greenery with the excitement of subtropical plants. The scene is set at the perimeter, for outside are clipped wavy hedges of pittosporum and eleagnus. A timber pergola over the entrance has a boat riding a sea of wisteria to whisk you away to far places. Once inside the visitor finds a lush tropical land where plants include a fan palm (*Cordyline australis*), huge palmate-leaved *Kalopanax septemlobus* and a bamboo grove. Mimosa (*Acacia dealbata*), Spanish broom (*Spartium junceum*) and pineapple broom (*Cytisus battandieri*) add flowers and scents. On the far wall is a huge rusting mill wheel 30 feet/9 metres high. This industrial relic was rescued from the local marble factory of 1860 when the building was demolished.

You may prefer the hot dry Mediterranean area in the centre of the garden, where euphorbias, kniphofias, prickly eryngiums, silybums and water-retaining succulents thrive alongside fine floaty stipas. Close by a playground is tucked in among small hillocks and a few birches that make a 'wood'.

Left Autumn in the garden of Bonnington Square is dominated by tangles of seed heads.

The garden is managed very well by local volunteers, plantspeople, artists and architects. It has had a great impact upon the neighbourhood and the ideas have spilled over to the streets surrounding the square.

ROOTS AND SHOOTS

SE11

Walnut Tree Walk is a pretty name for a place that leads to what was once the derelict, overgrown and polluted landscape of a former Civil Defence site in a deprived area of London not far from Waterloo station. Today the site is alive with flowers, butterflies, insects and children. The transformation is due to

Above In the gardens at Bonnington Square plants such as the dark hollyhock *Alcea rosea* 'Nigra' and teasels (*Dipsacus fullonum*) grow alongside willow herb (*Epilobium angustifolium*), the archetypal flower of London bomb sites.

the energies of local people and dedicated enthusiasts who rescued the ground.

Here is a place of wonderment for the many small children who visit. But it is more than that. The ½ acre site is now the home of Roots and Shoots, a charity that offers training in horticulture, conservation and carpentry as well as work experience to people aged sixteen to twenty-five who have learning difficulties. Here city children, their families and the older generations too can experience a totally different world.

It is amazing what has been fitted into this small garden. The Wildlife Garden has a pond with a small timber deck. There is a Summer Meadow with knapweed, field scabious, oxeye daisies, teasels, meadow cranesbill and wild marjoram. A hazel coppice explains a system used for over 1,000 years. The flowers in the borders include phlomis, verbascum and

several linked lakes. One is open, with two charming pergola-covered seating areas from which to see the myriad waterfowl: moorhens, coots, ducks, Canada geese, mallards and swans. Lower down are more pools, secret and secluded because of dense encircling foliage. Overhanging willows, a tall weeping ash, majestic poplars, plus rarities including a Caucasian wingnut (*Pterocarya fraxinifolia*) and the magenta-flowering Judas tree (*Cercis siliquastrum*), are thick with birds. Beside the chain of lakes, a sweeping meadow of rough-cut grass adds to the rural feeling of this part of the park.

But it is the Old English Garden, enclosed behind tall old brick walls, that is probably the park's most distinctive feature. Here the format is geometric with large clipped plants, mostly yews, in the shape of cubes, wedges, mounds and a high arch. These are aged and slightly misshapen, creating secret paths and hidden spaces and a romantic, old-fashioned atmosphere. This is a very child-friendly space.

Above The secluded wall garden, with clipped hedges, a pool and pretty summer flowers like scarlet oriental poppies, makes a charming summer retreat in Brockwell Park.

It is also a place for those who love flowers, for sudden open views reveal lushly planted beds. Spring beds of velvety wallflowers and tulips give way to the summer colour of herbaceous irises, aquilegias, delphiniums, poppies, lilies and leucanthemums, with ground-covering geraniums and bistorts lower down. There are roses of all sizes, including some small standards. Covering the high walls are many wisterias, one providing a tunnel walk, as well as climbing roses, hydrangeas, magnolias, clematis and vines. There are trees that include the cabbage gum (*Eucalyptus paucifolia* subsp. *niphophila*), the katsura tree (*Cercidiphyllum japonicum*), a gnarled black mulberry (*Morus nigra*) and *Clerodendrum trichotomum*, a deciduous shrub with pretty white flower clusters followed by blue fruits.

BURGESS PARK AND CHUMLEIGH MULTICULTURAL GARDENS
SE5

After the Second World War the Abercrombie Plan proposed creating new 'green lungs' for London, and Burgess Park was an important part of the scheme. Despite the growing values of property and land, the Greater London Council, strongly led by Lord Birkett, had the vision to make a large green space in a high-density built-up area of Southwark. To make this large public park of 135 acres, whole streets, industrial buildings, wharves and houses were bulldozed and a canal was filled in.

This large continuous green space, surrounded by urban concerns, is divided by a road, Wells Way, but the two parts of the park are connected by an underpass. Though work is not yet finished, and the park is still rather bleak and windswept, Groundwork Southwark has completed the landscaping of large areas. Almost four thousand trees have been planted. Paths and lighting have been installed, children's play areas built, sports pitches and a large lake for water sports put in place.

The expanse of green grass and maturing trees evokes the pastures and orchards that were here before the growing metropolis consumed everything in its path. It was the old Grand Surrey Canal, built at the start of the nineteenth century, that brought about the changes, by enabling materials to be brought easily to the district. Factories were built, needing people, who in turn needed homes and were crammed into mean terraces, without any space or greenery. By the early twentieth century there were almost 17,000 people living here, many unemployed.

To make space for the park, terraced houses were replaced by high-rise blocks. But a few old buildings were kept, among them some almshouses of 1821. This pretty spot was originally an 'asylum' for old ladies. Despite wartime damage, the buildings were restored and their gardens now form the Chumleigh Multicultural Gardens. Each is designed in the style of a garden from a different climate and culture: English, African, Oriental, Caribbean, Islamic and Mediterranean.

Unlikely plants are not merely surviving here, in the wrong climate but thriving as a result of the love and care they receive. They include a jelly palm (*Butia capitata*), Japanese bitter orange (*Poncirus trifoliata*), the Australian fuchsia (*Correa* 'Mannii'), the blue Mexican fan palm (*Brahea armata*), the paper mulberry from South-east Asia (*Broussonetia papyrifera*) and the rice paper plant (*Tetrapanax papyrifer*); these mix with tree ferns, gum trees, figs and even aloes. There are dry areas with cacti and succulents in the African and Caribbean Gardens and aromatic plants in the Mediterranean Garden. Rocks represent a mountainous landscape in the Oriental Garden and there is a glossily tiled pond at the centre of the Islamic Garden. All the plants are carefully and knowledgably tended and there are containers that are changed frequently to include associated bulbs and tender perennials.

There is also a communal vegetable and herb garden where those without gardens of their own may grow vegetables. The legendary Chumleigh Multicultural Gardens are fascinating, introducing the visitor to new ideas, and stimulating creativity; educational fun packs are offered for children. But they are also a place of quiet repose, where colours and fragrances wash over you, enabling you to leave the tensions of the city far away.

The Camberwell Beauty butterfly (*Vanessa antiopa*) came to the area with imported wood brought here by canal. It was adopted as a trademark by one of the local manufacturers, who used Royal Doulton tiles to make a large mosaic butterfly for its wall. During the war the butterfly was painted over to confuse the Luftwaffe. When the building was demolished in 1982, the tiles were carefully re-set on the wall of the public library and the butterfly is now the proud symbol of the park.

GREENWICH PARK
SE10

In 1433, Henry VI allowed the Duke of Gloucester, who had built himself a lodge, Bella Court, on the bank of the river, to enclose 200 acres of Blackheath, to be used as a deer park. On the Duke's death, Henry took over the lodge, which became Greenwich Palace, making this area the first of the royal parks. Henry VIII, Elizabeth I and Mary I were all born at Greenwich Palace. Henry married two of his wives at Greenwich and Elizabeth spent a lot of time there, arriving by gilded royal barge. James I employed Inigo Jones to build a Palladian house in the park for his queen, Anne of Denmark. The Queen's House still stands and is famed for its elegant proportions.

Top Looking from Chumleigh Multicultural Gardens' Mediterranean Garden to the jelly palm (*Butia capitata*) in the Islamic Garden.
Centre The South American passion flower (*Passiflora caerulea*).
Bottom Mediterranean *Acanthus spinosus*.

During the Commonwealth, Cromwell's men wrecked the palace and cut down many of the trees in the park. In 1675 Charles II decided to replace the palace with a building to complement the Queen's House but the building was never completed. He energetically replanted the park and had the area landscaped.

The initial design was done by Le Nôtre, designer of Versailles, who probably never actually came to the park, but designed by post. Three hundred elm trees were planted to make fine straight avenues that were intended to focus upon the Queen's House but did not quite do so. The elms have gone but some ancient sweet chestnuts from that time are still alive, characterized by their rutted spiralling bark. The straight Blackheath Avenue at the crest of the hill is lined by horse chestnuts and probably follows the intended geometric layout. It is thickly crossed at right angles by lines of sweet chestnuts.

During the reign of William and Mary the palace was demolished and a new building completed that was to be the Royal Naval Hospital. The job of designing it was given to Sir Christopher Wren, who created two matching but separate buildings, with a wide axial space between them so that, from the river, the Queen's House was seen to be central. The hospital subsequently became the Royal Naval College and, very recently, the home of Greenwich University. In 1809, colonnades were built on either side of the Queen's House to connect the buildings that ultimately became the world-famous National Maritime Museum.

Sir Christopher Wren was also commissioned by Charles II to build the Royal Observatory on top of the hill in Greenwich Park for the Astronomer Royal, the Reverend John Flamsteed. Here in Flamsteed House a suspended red time-ball is still hauled up every day so as to fall at precisely 1.00 p.m., this being the old means of signalling the time to shipmasters in the Port of London, so that they could set their ships'

chronometers. And in 1884, following the settling of international arguments about longitude, the meridian line dividing the western hemisphere from the eastern hemisphere was established upon the site. There are many more historical connections here to fascinate visitors, who can then stroll down the green slopes of the park to the National Maritime Museum for further enrichment.

Northwards from the observatory, the parkland sweeps down to the River Thames, facing what was once the flat marshland of the Isle of Dogs and the distant heights of Epping Forest – a fit setting for the superb buildings. But today the massive undertaking of Canary Wharf grossly dominates the view. However, the sight is still one of the finest in London, as it was in Wren's day. To see all this beauty, as Wren did, from the tip of the Isle of Dogs, follow the foot tunnel from near the old tea clipper, the *Cutty Sark*, as it leads beneath the Thames to Island Gardens. Better still, arrive by boat, in the tradition of Elizabeth I, and see this magnificent view from the river.

If entering the park from the lower level at St Mary's Gate, the visitor will find a fragrant herb garden, redolent of summer days and a reminder of the value of herbs in past times, when smells had to be camouflaged and herbs were thought to be the key to health. Up the hill, past the Observatory and near the Ranger's House, is a large semi-circular garden crammed with a hundred or so different roses; beyond this is a luscious rhododendron dell. Also high up, and south-east of the Bower Avenue, is a lake, popular with waterfowl and children, and a little-frequented wilderness of 13 acres, where fallow deer hide from view.

Ornamental deciduous trees in the park include a tulip tree (*Liriodendron tulipifera*), paper-bark birch (*Betula papyrifera*), Chinese yellow wood (*Cladrastis lutea*), Pride of India (*Koelreuteria paniculata*), foxglove tree (*Paulownia tomentosa*) and red oaks (*Quercus rubra*) from the United States. Some of the ornamental trees have not grown to their full shape, because during the Second World War their heights were reduced to clear the line of fire for anti-aircraft guns. Making up for such imperfection is the Flower Garden up the hill near the lake, where spanning cedars and stately conifers grow from smooth grass, set with many flower beds. These are filled from spring to summer, starting with bulbs and coming to a climax with dahlias.

Right Looking down from the Royal Observatory in Greenwich Park to the classically spacious Naval History Museum, the colonnades and the Queen's House – and, behind, the crammed verticals of Canary Wharf.

PLEASURE GROUNDS AND COMMONS

FROM BLACKHEATH TO WIMBLEDON

PLEASURE GROUNDS AND COMMONS
From Blackheath to Wimbledon

Blackheath, Crystal Palace Park, Dulwich Park, Lesnes Abbey Woods, Oxleas Wood, Maryon Park and Maryon Wilson Park, Peckham Rye Park, Choumert Square, Horniman Museum, Eltham Palace, Hall Place, Beckenham Place Park, Battersea Park, Wimbledon Common, Cannizaro Park

The rural heights of south London, from Blackheath to Wimbledon Common, are as valued as Epping Forest and Hampstead Heath across the river. Such places are the 'natural gardens' of the capital. They offer urban children – and adults – the chance to see the habitats of plants, animals and insects, or places to go fishing, tree climbing, running, cycling or playing sports on grassland.

As well as the wild places, in south-east London there are many Victorian parks, enhancing the well-being of the surrounding communities as they were intended to do when they were created in the nineteenth century. But today they are no longer dominated by formal flower-filled beds. Reflecting the increasing public enthusiasm for urban wildlife, Beckenham Place Park, for instance, is one of many public parks that have areas where the grass is cut infrequently, to foster native plants. Likewise 'corridors' for wildlife have been established on old railway land at the Horniman Museum.

In a modern initiative to develop the green spaces available to the public, the Green Chain Walk on the south bank of the River Thames was established in 1977. Four London boroughs, Bexley, Bromley, Greenwich and Lewisham, co-operated to pioneer a long-distance trackway of over forty miles of open land made by linking green spaces. There are three starting points, at Thamesmead, Erith and the Thames Barrier. Among the places it takes in are Lesnes Abbey Woods, Beckenham Place Park, Maryon Wilson Park and Crystal Palace Park, and it passes through allotments, school playgrounds, public common land and fragments of ancient forest such as Oxleas Wood. *En route* are areas with a fascinating history, Sites of Special Scientific Interest, gardens awash with flowers and fine trees, and simple places of beauty with wonderful views. Stops worth making along the way include the gardens of Eltham Palace and those of nearby Hall Place, both of which have a unique character determined by their association with remarkable historic buildings.

Some of the parks also offer other, more worldly pleasures: Crystal Palace Park was designed around the remarkable glass structure made for the Great Exhibition of 1851, and Battersea Park, which, a century later had its Festival of Britain Pleasure Gardens. And all over this part of London there are gardens made brilliant by flowers, like the tiny domestic gardens of Choumert Square and Cannizaro Park with its bedding.

Heaths and commons, wild areas and gardened spaces – each is special in its way, and we take pleasure in them all.

BLACKHEATH
SE3

This open, empty, rounded hill overlooking the Thames valley was once wooded, but from Roman times it was recognized as a place for settlement, because of the commanding views all around. After the Romans, Saxons and Danes also left their imprints here. The heath is linked later with Wat Tyler, leader of the Peasants' Revolt, whose supporters assembled here before marching on London in 1381. Henry V was welcomed at Blackheath after his success at the Battle of Agincourt. Henry VII defeated the Cornish rebels here in 1497. Henry VIII staged a fabulous pageant to greet his new bride, Anne of Cleves. In the eighteenth century John Wesley and George Whitefield held Revivalist meetings on the heath.

Blackheath has sombre connotations, for it was a burial place for plague victims. The name Blackheath probably derives from the Black Death. Because of its association with the plague, it was never built over and has always been common land. When London expanded in the eighteenth century, fine, classically styled mansions, such as the crescent of the Paragon and Morden College, were built around the perimeter. The village of Blackheath down the hill from the heath was begun then, and some cottages from the eighteenth century have survived. Always rather genteel, the area has attracted the professional middle classes. Famous inhabitants include the astronomer Sir Arthur Eddington, the philosopher John Stuart Mill, the novelist Nathaniel Hawthorne and the composer Charles Gounod.

Pages 210–211 Flowering perennials are fitted into the ancient wall buttresses as part of the superb herbaceous beds in the former moat at Eltham Palace.

Page 213 High above Dulwich Village, allotments look out over London, with upturned bottles rattling in the wind acting as bird-scarers.

Left An approaching storm threatens the calm of Blackheath.

Some unusual native grasses and plants grow in the dark acidic soil. But the heath remains more valued as an ideal expanse for fairs, fun and sports such as archery, kite flying and flying model aeroplanes.

CRYSTAL PALACE PARK
SE26

The sensational glass conservatory that held the Great Exhibition of 1851 in Hyde Park, a fantasy of glass and iron designed by Joseph Paxton, was removed after the exhibition closed to a site on Sydenham Hill, south of the river. The building was reconstructed on the southern slopes of the hill, overlooking the Kent landscape and visible for miles among the spreading suburbs of Victorian London, and this park was designed around it.

The palace covered an area of 2000 by 400 feet/610 by 121 metres. A thousand labourers were employed to prepare the ground for the new park. Over 50,000 red pelargoniums were ordered. Immaculate beds were maintained with strongly coloured flower schemes containing calceolarias, lobelias, petunias, heliotrope, verbenas and salvias. At the time it was confidently asserted that 'the Crystal Palace Gardens will do more to encourage a taste for gardening and a love of flowers among the lower classes, than even the London Parks.'

Like all the best Victorian parks, Crystal Palace Park was intended not only to delight but also to instruct: there were firmly held ideas of 'improving' the public. In pursuit of these, some of the lifelike but inaccurate full-sized dinosaurs from the Great Exhibition were transferred from Hyde Park to Sydenham to illustrate pre-history. Futhermore, when Paxton was called upon to lay out the new park on Sydenham Hill he included facsimiles of natural rock formations, and, advised by Professor Richard Owen, placed some real rocks to illustrate the geological formations of limestone, chalk beds, millstone grit, ironstone, coal measures and sandstone. Today, on the Geological Time Trail beside a boating lake, the dinosaurs can be seen lurking among the trees on the islands or in the waters around them. A mighty iguanadon gazes threateningly from the undergrowth, a glaring pterodactyl contemplates flight, reptilian amphibians are about to crawl out of the swamp and a hostile megalosaurus stands still, supremely sure of itself. They can frighten nobody who has seen the film *Jurassic Park*, but the time travel idea is fun and predates Disneyland by over a hundred years. There is a story that while the monsters were being built, on New Year's Eve 1851, some members of the Royal Society partook of dinner inside one of them.

At Sydenham the palace was for many years the centre of a popular amusement park. Already by the late nineteenth century the company that ran it was suffering financial troubles. An ode in *Punch* magazine entitled 'Reduced Circumstances' spelt out the decline:

How they've allowed me to get impecunious,
    Think of my Rose Shows!
And what are you going
To do with your Shahs and your Emperors in future?
    For when I am gone
There'll be nothing worth showing.

However, the palace survived until 1936 when the glass building, by now shabby, rusting and undervalued, caught fire and could not be saved. It is said that the fire could be seen as far away as Brighton and that rivers of melted glass ran down the hill; so in its last hours it regained some of its former grandeur.

The foundations of the massive terrace are still to be seen, showing exactly how large the whole thing was. Standing there is a dwarfing experience. The wide, imposing flights of steps that lead to the upper terrace are still flanked by copies of an Egyptian sphinx in the Louvre Museum in Paris. But the plinths

that run along the balustrade of the terrace are now empty where they once held statuary representing the Empire as well as ornamental vases and urns.

The Italian gardens on the lower terrace, designed by Paxton, are long gone but a walled garden at the crest of the hill has azaleas and remarkably colourful bedding, still with a Victorian flavour. Some fine old trees are dotted around the park, including English oak, a large weeping beech, cypresses, pines, monkey puzzles and an avenue of London plane trees.

Today Crystal Palace Park is still very popular, and its 200 acres of potential are much used. Where once fantastic spectacles such as firework displays, music festivals and balloon launching attracted thousands of people, today there are still festivals and fireworks, though small kites replace the giant balloons. Concerts are held in the concert bowl and as well as the boating lake, the park has a zoo, a miniature railway, a dry-

Above On an island in the lake at Crystal Palace Park lurk some threatening but inaccurate winged monsters from the dinosaur age.

ski slope, a museum and a large restored maze of hornbeam. Outstanding sports facilities, including a large sports hall and youth centre, draw the crowds again and there is even a place for the French game *pétanque*.

However, the park is seriously in need of a facelift. A competition was held by the local authority to find a designer who could interpret the spirit of the park rather than simply restoring the original design; it was won by the landscaper Kathryn Gustafson. In anticipation, an attractive new network of paths has been built with a grant from the Heritage Lottery Fund. Gustafson's innovative plans for a matrix of mixed perennials will be carried out but the work has had to be phased and the whole scheme cannot be implemented until more funds become available. Paxton's rhododendron collection has been recreated by studying a bill of quantities now in the British Library and by using rhododendrons that were available in 1850. As a fascinating contrast, another area concentrates upon only modern cultivars of rhododendrons.

DULWICH PARK

SE21

Originally the land that is now Dulwich Park was part of the common land of the Manor of Dulwich. In the early seventeenth century the manor was bought by the actor Edward Alleyn, who subsequently used it to endow the school that eventually became Dulwich College. In 1890, the college generously presented all 70 acres to the public.

Although Dulwich is a fine Victorian park, it is the trees that make it such a draw for garden lovers. Many remarkable trees were already established before 1890. Visitors can see the Kentucky coffee tree (*Gymnocladus dioica*), Cappadocian maple (*Acer cappadocicum*), Japanese pagoda tree (*Sophora japonica*) and tree of heaven (*Ailanthus altissima*). There are also superb specimens of Turkey oak, Atlantic cedar and copper beech, as

well as natives like ancient oaks that mark lost field boundaries, white birches and plane trees.

The circular road, partly open to cars, offers alternative means of exploring. There are various items of transport for hire, and great fun can be had pedalling around on one of the recumbent bikes – perhaps hauling a trailer full of youngsters.

The 3-acre boating lake is awash with waterfowl including coots, moorhens, teal, tufted and mandarin ducks and mallards, plus the occasional visiting heron. More birds can be seen in the nineteenth-century aviary. The park is very child-friendly, having a playground, two ecological sites and a nature trail. As a community park it is concerned with people, and the Parks Rangers Service, run by Southwark Council for five major parks in the borough, mans the visitors' centre and is generally there to help. The rangers also get involved with community groups, events and nature conservation.

The Drought-tolerant Garden is the creation of the Parks Rangers Service. Some funding and support came from Thames Water and Southwark Council. Supporting the Rangers Service's philosophy of 'Think globally, act locally' – that is, aim at an environmental approach to gardening – this is a garden that needs no watering. The drought-resistant plants are mainly from the Mediterranean. Many of them – artemisias, santolina and lavender – have silver-grey foliage that looks lovely in full sunshine. Evergreens such as cistus, helianthemums, euphorbias and rosemary contribute flowers as well as attractive foliage, while succulents which thrive by conserving water in their fleshy leaves include sedums, sempervivums and crassulas. In the south-east of England generally summers are drier than they were, and water conservation has become an important issue. By showing visitors how successful such an approach can be Dulwich Park encourages the use of drought-tolerant plants in domestic gardens.

Other park features include wonderful azaleas and rhododendrons, visited regularly at one time by Queen Mary.

Masses of flowering bulbs are a joy in spring and there is a garden thoughtfully planned for physically disabled people.

LESNES ABBEY WOODS
SE2

'Will no one rid me of this turbulent priest?' The famous cry of Henry II, referring to Archbishop Thomas à Becket, lies behind the building of Lesnes Abbey. It is thought that Richard de Luci was among those who took Henry at his word: though not actually one of the perpetrators, he seems to have had some involvement with the murder of Becket at Canterbury Cathedral. For the rest of his life, fearing for his immortal soul, he tried to make amends and in 1178, as an act of penance, he donated land and funds to build an Augustinian abbey. The abbey was not prosperous, being burdened by the expense of responsibility for managing the dykes and river walls of Plumstead marshes in the Abbey lands. In any case, the shadow of Henry VIII hung over its future and in 1524 Cardinal Wolsey dissolved it under papal licence.

The site suffered centuries of neglect, and for seventy years, after the walls of the dykes gave way to the Thames, it was swallowed up by marshland. Then in 1930 it was bought by the London County Council and laid out for parkland as part of the Green Belt.

The ruins that remain today are mostly low walls and a neatly displayed layout, managed by the borough of Bexley. The aisles of the abbey can be seen and the refectory, kitchens and dormitory are clearly marked, but only one arch still stands. Any items of interest have been removed to the safety of museums including the Victoria and Albert Museum.

Top A golden-leaved form of the Indian bean tree in full flower in early summer in Dulwich Park.
Centre Glossy red haws add colour in early autumn.
Bottom Also in autumn, a reddening vine.

The real prize here is that much of the 215 acres of parkland contains indigenous planting. The tidy level bit around the abbey is beautifully kept, with an old mulberry tree leaning into the wind and, around the old stone ruins, a collection of ferns, including spleenworts, polypodies, hart's tongue and maidenhair ferns. Records kept by the monks refer to medicinal herbs grown there, such as the small wild daffodil (*Narcissus pseudonarcissus*), every part of which is a powerful emetic. It was known as the Lent lily and the sixteenth-century herbalist John Gerard recorded it as growing everywhere in Britain, in sun, shade, damp or dryish spots. These tiny daffodils, found now mostly in Wales and Cumbria, still thrive in Lesnes Abbey Woods and, according to the naturalist Richard Mabey, this is 'one of the nearest colonies of authentically wild flowers to London'. It is wonderful to see masses of small daffodils in spring and know that they have

Above Spring in Lesnes Abbey Woods is heady with the fragrance of deep blue English bluebells.

service tree and wild cherry, with many native flowering plants, fungi, bluebells, wood anemones and celandines. Coppicing with standards was practised right up to the Second World War, as many of the trees show. There has been a fight to preserve the wood and save it from road development. At present, because of lack of money, it has been reprieved. Like Lesnes Abbey Woods, it includes a section of the Green Chain Walk. Other paths criss-cross the woods and on one there is an eighteenth-century folly, Severndroog Castle, built in 1784.

MARYON PARK AND MARYON WILSON PARK

SE7

Here two parks, donated at the turn of the twentieth century for the public by the Maryon Wilson family, father and son, are joined together, though cut across by Thorntree Road.

Maryon Park is a deeply set, intimate park within two hanging wooded banks. The Green Chain Walk runs along the ridges on both sides. The ground rises so steeply that timber steps are essential. On the northern ridge is Cox's Hill, a large grassy mound that used to have amazing views from east to west along the river and in the days of sail was a lookout post; but the shrubs would need to be drastically thinned for the view to be seen now. At the time of writing it has been fenced off because the paths are virtually clay slides, becoming more lethal with every drop of rain. A hundred years ago there was a Victorian summerhouse on top; today there is a ramshackle replacement, a den built by local boys, pleased with their secret site.

Maryon Wilson Park is just as greenly refreshing as its relative. One of the prettiest small parks in south London, it was laid out after the First World War, having before then

grown on this hilly wooded landscape for centuries. Then, later in spring the ridges and ditches are filled by carpets of white wood anemones, followed by deep blue fragrant English bluebells. The trees are mostly oak and birch with old sweet chestnuts and some wild cherries. Woodpeckers and warblers are some of the many birds happily satisfied by this woodland habitat. Adding to the interest of this magical place are the fossils that have been found here, of which a display, donated by the Tertiary Research Group, can be seen in the café.

OXLEAS WOOD

SE9

Nearby Oxleas Wood, part of Shooters Hill, is another ancient woodland, which dates back to the last Ice Age. It has great botanical diversity and has been declared a Site of Special Scientific Interest. There are old trees here, such as the wild

Above An old mulberry tree leans almost parallel with the ground in front of the twelfth-century walls of Lesnes Abbey.

temporarily provided ground for allotments. But there has been no attempt to formalize it, and the atmosphere is set by the steeply uneven terrain with wooded groves, rising grass slopes and the little stream gently meandering through.

Large trees of hornbeam, lime, willow and oak make shady places and old hawthorn hedges have grown to small tree height. Blackthorn, white with blossom in early spring, elders, dog roses and tangles of bramble grow as randomly as nature intended. In spring areas of sandy soil are touched with gorse yellow and the edges of the woods are luminous with primroses. Youngsters enjoy the small enclosed area for domestic animals, ponies, deer, sheep, bantams and peafowl.

The Romans once lived on the site of the parks, in a fortified camp on the heights, and left behind them pieces of well-preserved pottery. The area was also associated with highwaymen. More recently, the spirit of the parks, with their unforgettable rustling trees. was captured in the 1960s Antonioni film *Blow Up*.

PECKHAM RYE PARK

SE15

The common at Peckham Rye has the charm of a wilderness, even though it is very well used. As a protected open space, it dates from the fourteenth century and it has survived takeover bids on and off since the mid-eighteenth century; parish records reveal the strength of public feeling whenever the land was threatened by enclosure. Eventually the common ended up in the hands of the Metropolitan Board of Works, saved for the foreseeable future.

The existence of the adjacent 50-acre Peckham Rye Park is due to a campaign that successfully proposed adding farmland to the common when it became available in 1894. The common was no longer big enough for the community and an extra park was needed to spread the load.

By the late twentieth century the park was ailing, having become run down, a place that was no longer enticing and that fostered vandalism. Now, however, once again, local intervention is saving the park. Persuaded by the Friends of Peckham Rye Park, the Parks Rangers Service has committed itself to restoring this valuable park and has come up trumps by securing a grant from the Heritage Lottery Fund. Designs were devised by Chris Blandford Environmental Landscape Planners, in consultation with local people, and now stage one of these improvements has begun.

This is essentially a Victorian park and will remain so. The existing Victorian layout and atmosphere are to be retained but subtly improved. Aims include repairing existing features, like the old bridges, paths and benches – practicalities that are crucial to a park's success. Established but rather shabby theme gardens are in line for restoration as well.

The Sexby Garden, formerly the Old English Garden, has a pergola-covered walk, with crazy-paving paths, perennials, roses and wisteria-clad pergolas, all enclosed by walls of yew. The old Rock Garden is looking sad and in need of redefining because many feet have cut through between the shrubs and flattened or broken them. The Japanese Garden is rather English, being slightly overgrown; it has a pretty stream running through it, featuring ponds, but without attention the banks get spoiled and the watercourses clogged. Restoring the American Garden, mostly planted with North American trees and shrubs, is also on the list of jobs to be done.

Among the assets of the park is a quiet secluded area where rough-cut grass encourages native plants and fosters wildlife. Fine tree groups of eucalyptus with magnolias, acers, specimen conifers and a taxodium lift the spirits. And there are some excellent sports facilities, including pitches for football and cricket, tennis courts, bowling greens and a popular adventure playground resembling a child-sized assault course.

CHOUMERT SQUARE
SE15

Close to Peckham Rye there is an unusual street of small Victorian houses that, instead of being traditional 'back to backs', are actually 'front to fronts'. There is no room for backyards, so all attention is focused upon the fronts, and the mini-gardens of these facing rows of tiny houses – there are forty-six altogether – nestle alongside each other, with plants and flowers cascading on to a central path.

Each garden is highly individual, revealing personal passions. But the gardens overlap with great abandon and no discord, and their intimacy creates a unified charm, while their lack of conformity is very much part of their appeal.

The gardens are awash with luscious flower colour, well organized with hedging and summer bedding or overflowing with climbing roses, clematis and honeysuckle growing above lavender, campanulas, delphiniums, sedums, irises, pinks and geraniums. They are so pretty that when shown on BBC television they were described as a 'floral canyon'. Most have tiny paved areas for a small table and a couple of chairs, set among the flowers.

George Choumert was an émigré from Lorraine who arrived here at the end of the eighteenth century. Not much is known about the rows of houses that bear his name, but they may have been 'thrown up' for navvies building the railway in the 1820s – a possibility attested to by a disintegrating plaque that dates some cottages at 1821, a date also found scratched under wallpaper in one of the cottages. The Ordnance Survey map of 1860 does not show the houses, but that may well be because they were the 'pre-fabs' of their day. Possibly more houses were added for employees at the adjacent Victorian factory.

In the 1930s the owner of Tilt estate bought the cottages almost by accident, when they were thrown in as part of a job lot along with her intended purchase. It was she, the late Mrs

Harvey, who saved them from destruction by bulldozer after some suffered during the bombing of the Second World War; she described them as 'Chelsea in Peckham'. They were later restored and most are now privately owned.

HORNIMAN MUSEUM
SE23

Frederick John Horniman MP, of Horniman's Tea, was a great world traveller and, like most of us when abroad, found buying souvenirs of his travels irresistible. With a good eye and fascination with natural history as well as arts and crafts, he built up an outstanding and idiosyncratic collection. Initially he displayed these artefacts in his own house and opened the collection to the public three times a week, but the enthusiasm of the public response led him to found a museum. For this he commissioned a design in the best Art Nouveau tradition by C. Harrison Townsend. An elegant glass conservatory from the family home was transferred and rebuilt behind the museum. In 1901 the museum and its 21 acres of gardens were generously gifted to the London County Council.

The land around the museum lies on a steep ridge, over 300 feet/120 metres above the level of the Thames. There are superb views on both sides, to the north of St Paul's, the City and the Northern Heights beyond or, looking the other way, of the North Downs and towards Kent. The ridge has been landscaped partly by maintaining the sweeping grass slopes and partly by terracing with brick and stone, which allowed the Sunken Garden to be viewed from above on two levels.

The gardeners have used the Sunken Garden as an opportunity for change every year. Recently the plan has been to create a

flamboyant garden with summer bedding that is strikingly colour charged. Glowing zinnias and helichrysums establish the overall vibrancy. Tender perennials mix with annuals to create a vividly exotic look. There are dahlias in all colours, golden rudbeckias and deep purple heliotropes beside dark blue salvias and wine-red furry spires of amaranthus. Tall flaming cannas and the wide-spreading dark red leaves of the caster-oil plant (*Ricinus*) stand above the deep plum-red and purple-black of orach and perilla foliage. Other edibles are included for their colour, including Swiss chard and ornamental corn. In the central rectangle the fluffy colours of celmisias are startling. They were ringed with richly foliaged banana plants but these were stolen within the first week of setting out. Contending with vandalism is a constant struggle for gardeners in public parks and it is disappointing for them when their careful planning goes awry. Everything here has been grown from seed saved by the gardeners themselves, and nothing bought in. Kevin, who has gardened here for eighteen years, maintains this area with care and passion.

Opposite Richly coloured cannas in the grounds of the Horniman Museum. *Above right* In a fascinating annual flower scheme in the sunken garden at the Horniman Museum, texture, especially that of the fluffy celmisias, is almost as important as colour.

The gardens cater for everyone. There are quiet areas and 'kickabout' areas, games places and even a dog field. Animal enclosures with bantams, guinea fowl, cranes, wallabies and rabbits attract young families. The sundial is fun, as it depends upon a person to act as gnomon. The bandstand provides a stage for every type of concert in summer while the Dutch barn acts as an education centre or gallery for exhibitions.

It is fitting that the museum should be accompanied by a collection of exotic trees from around the world. They include the dawn redwood from California, the ginkgo from the temples of south China, the deodar cedar that grows in the western Himalayas, a tall swamp cypress from the Gulf of Mexico, and western hemlock, which grows in western North America; the spindle trees are Asian, the snake bark maples were discovered in China and the tulip trees are North American. More exotica will soon be growing in the gardens: there is an exciting new proposal to make an ethno-botanical garden that would perfectly complement the museum.

An extra strip of land, formerly railway land, was added in 1973. This is now used as a wildlife area, where three nature trails follow routes shown in the printed guides.

ELTHAM PALACE
SE9

The grounds of Eltham Palace are unlike those of any other garden in London, largely because they belong to a house that is unique, being part medieval royal palace and part the glamorous 1930s home of Stephen and Virginia Courtauld, styled with the elegance of the period. The palace saw great days when it was favoured by Henry VIII and it was to see great days again almost four hundred years later when the Courtaulds took over.

The Courtaulds bought the remains of the moated building and gardens in 1933, restoring the medieval hall with its fine hammerbeam roof and commissioning the architects Seely and Paget to integrate the old palace buildings into a modern, comfortable and chic home. Externally the newer buildings are restrained, but inside the reverse is true. The interior is gloriously and boldly designed in the French Art Deco style, that was the cutting edge of 1930s fashion. Executed with integrity and judgment, the design is uncompromising, and yet the house is congenial and comfortable – qualities that are too often forgotten in the pursuit of fashion. The décor says a lot about the owners – their money, but also their confidence, their warmth and their sense of style.

The moated palace is set within a large area of parkland with open views over London. The visitor approaches over a fifteenth-century stone bridge that crosses the moat. Both Courtaulds were extremely keen on the garden and paid it the same detailed attention as they had the interior of the house. New gardens were laid out in 1937 incorporating the medieval walls. The architects co-operated with Thomas Mawson, a leading landscape designer at the time. Before Mawson's Arts and Crafts plan was completed, however, the Second World War intervened, bringing work on the garden to an abrupt stop, and much of the garden was never actually properly gardened.

After 1945 the estate was maintained as a park, first by the Ministry of Defence and subsequently by the Army Education Corps, which stayed until 1992. Until then the Royal Parks had kept things ticking over, but English Heritage was already on site, caring for the Great Hall, so it took on the garden as well. Now that the restoration inside is complete, English Heritage has turned its attention to the garden, with a view to recovering its Arts and Crafts character. A senior gardener, Jane Cordingley, was appointed in 1999, with a staff of three; there are also, fortunately, twenty-four enthusiastic volunteers. Despite the garden's age, because it was never finished it is really in its infancy.

The Cascade Rock Garden can be seen from the house, across the moat. Water tumbles over water-worn limestone from Westmorland, as planned by Mawson. (The practice of stripping the top off limestone pavements, common in Victorian days, is seriously frowned on today.) The gardening team has had to

Above left Stately cannas and deep red dahlias mingle with soft grey artemisia foliage in the garden at Eltham Palace.
Above right Tall *Verbena bonariensis* is invaluable in the late summer garden.

hand-weed all the ground elder from the rockery. And they are still pursuing bindweed. But it is all worth it, to allow the spread of alpines and acers that trail over rock surfaces.

A living record of the Courtauld days is a number of unusual ornamental specimen trees, some of which were gifts from the royal family. Amongst these are an Indian bean tree (*Catalpa bignonioides*), a tulip tree (*Liriodendron tulipifera*), a walnut (*Juglans regia*) and a bay tree (*Laurus nobilis*).

While Stephen Courtauld raised orchids in the glasshouse, Ginnie concentrated on roses. The sunken Rose Garden and attached garden 'rooms' were completed by the Courtaulds but needed overhauling. The Rose Garden has been replanted with cultivars of the 1930s such as Hybrid Teas and fragrant Hybrid Musks including apricot-pink *Rosa* 'Felicia' and soft peach *R.* 'Buff Beauty'. The garden rooms are enclosed by clipped hollies and, inside, flowering shrubs mingle with herbaceous perennials and spring bulbs.

Beside the house a triangular herb garden on the terrace has been appropriately and imaginatively interpreted with geometric precision. This is the work of John Watkins of English Heritage. A latticed parterre is filled with flat carpet thymes and acaenas, ornamented with spikes of *Kniphofia caulescens* and the soft velvet textures of *Salvia officinalis* 'Purpurascens'. Along one side are some Ionic columns that act as a pergola. These were salvaged from the Bank of England in the 1930s.

A long stretch of lawn replaces the old moat on the south side of the house. Beside it, along the bank at the foot of the upper terrace wall, is a herbaceous border 120 yards/100 metres long. Designed by Isabelle van Groeningen with texture and colour in mind, it looks wonderful from spring to September. It can be seen from above, on the 1930s wooden bridge that crosses the moat and leads to wide paths mown in meadow grass. Standing on the bridge, turn to look back at the house.

A new bed was made this year, based upon a flagrantly colourful theme. It was devised by Jane Cordingley, using cannas, red dahlias and eucomis with unusual nicotianas. Its sensational character reflects the bold interior design of the house and it has been a huge success.

Near by in Eltham is Avery Hill Park, which is famous for its Winter Garden, housed in a majestic conservatory. It is now owned by Greenwich University but is rather dusty and dreary: such things are horribly costly to maintain.

HALL PLACE
BEXLEY, KENT

In 1537 a former Lord Mayor of London, Sir John Champneys, built a magnificent Jacobean mansion at Hall Place, using stone from an old monastery. In 1649 a totally different brick addition extended the house, adding to the unique character of the building we see today. Following many tenancies and use eventually as a Victorian school, in the Second World War the United States Army made the house its home, using it for a top-secret Ultra code-breaking project. Now it houses the public library and Local Studies Museum Centre.

The black-and-white chequerboard effect of the original hall, using knapped flint and Kentish ragstone, makes an unusual backdrop for the gardens. Run by Bexley Council, these are maintained to a very high standard, including spring and summer bedding that is far more imaginative than that of many public gardens. The 16 acres of land are planned with the public in mind, leaving some valued open space while also offering many different gardens for the appreciation of those who enjoy plants and flowers.

The many gardens include a large traditional rose garden, planted in Elizabethan style, and an enclosed herb garden, with brick paths and boxed beds, filled with medicinal and culinary herbs, all labelled in Braille. Another unexpected sight is a turf maze, not old like the one at Saffron Walden, Essex, but recently made and irresistible to young children. At the top of the garden, running beside the road, is a turfed walk between two parallel herbaceous borders that are well stocked and rhythmically decorative, planted for colour, form and texture.

But it is the Topiary Garden that stays in the memory, not because it is old but because it is relatively young, and rather

Right The topiary Queen's Beasts, planted in 1953 for the Queen's coronation, could be mistaken for furry teddy bears when seen from behind.

unexpected in this informal age. Some dark green clipped yews make abstract groups set against the chequered house wall. They are designed with geometric simplicity: cone shapes and concentric discs, set on plinths, are surrounded by simple cubes and dome shapes. The fun starts where a regiment of the Queen's Beasts are ranked in a line along a path at right angles to the house. Planted for the coronation of Elizabeth II in 1953, these yews have been pruned and trained to form heraldic figures from the Royal Coats of Arms. Here are the Lion of England, the Welsh Griffin of Edward I, the Falcon of the Plantagenets, the Black Bull of Clarence, the White Lion of Mortimer, the Yale of Beaufort (a horse with tusks, horns and an elephant's tail), the White Greyhound of Richmond, the Red Dragon of Wales, the Hanoverian White Horse and the Scottish Unicorn. They stand still, facing front, as if waiting for inspection.

The River Cray slowly meanders through the area, dividing the site in two. The 'second half' has a different identity, being mostly given to an open expanse of grass, with tree clumps and specimen trees. A small rock area, to my mind the weakest part of the garden, has heathers and alpine plants. Although it includes some very pretty helianthemums, I feel that these are less effective against grass than in a stone or gravel garden, and that this rather isolated spot somehow looks too artificial. But I am being picky. Hall Place garden is much admired and frequently and deservedly wins awards. It is a pity that the A2 road is so close, because at times it rather disturbs the peace.

BECKENHAM PLACE PARK

KENT

This sixteenth-century parkland, covering 214 acres, includes ancient woodland and wild flower meadows, and has an old drovers' road cutting across the site, as well as a far newer railway line, where sometimes on a Sunday you might see a re-routed Eurostar train hastening to France. It is the old undulating woodland with native trees that captures the imagination, but there are also a few enclosed formal flower gardens. The Borough of Lewisham cares for the park very well and continues to protect and develop the region.

A majestic Portland stone mansion still stands high on the crest of the hill, surveying the rolling landscape below. It was built in the eighteenth century for a rather rascally local merchant and MP, John Cator. For all his dubious reputation, he wins points for delighting in the estate and planting many trees. As an enthusiastic amateur horticulturist, it seems that at one time he entertained the Swedish botanist Linnaeus here. Reflecting his interest in botany, today the house has a nature centre.

There are nature walks and wild flower meadows are being created and studied. The Friends of Beckenham Park are very active. The park was recognized early as a very people-friendly place: indeed, the first municipal golf course was established here, utilizing the natural contours of the land.

The Green Chain Walk crosses the park. It is clearly signposted and this is quite a hilly section. The narrow Ravensbrook stream is easily crossed and the scenery opens into clearings where sweeps of meadow grass offer fine views or it passes through woodland, between banks worn down by centuries of travellers. A fine collection of trees can be found amongst the plantations, including sessile and pedunculate oaks, many sweet chestnuts and collections of swamp cypress and black mulberry, as well as groups of Atlas cedars (*Cedrus atlantica*) with Persian ironwood (*Parrotia persica*).

BATTERSEA PARK

SW11

Battersea Park was created out of Battersea Fields, an area that was frequently flooded but had a few market gardens known for selling bunches of asparagus. Otherwise nothing redeemed

this rough place of roustabout behaviour, drinking booths, fortune-tellers and a weekly fair. A local cleric, the Reverend Robert Eden, was concerned about the state of his parishioners and their appalling living conditions, and wrote to the prime minister, suggesting that by building a park they could 'implant feelings which are now deadened by dirt, by drink and by discomfort'. And so, in 1846, the Commission for Improving the Metropolis bought the land, drained it and provided a landscaped public park, laid out by Sir James Pennethorne. They made a large lake with a cascade, and undulating ground at one end for a subtropical garden that in its day was famed abroad. The landscaping was intended to be 'gardenesque', to look casually natural, with meandering drives and walks, a serpentine lake and

Above left A team of fine horses, entered in the commercial carthorse class, seen at the Golden Jubilee London Harness Horse Parade in Battersea Park.
Above right Henry Moore's stone *Three Standing Figures*, permanently sited in the park since the Battersea Park Open Air Sculpture Exhibition of 1948.

uneven ground. But there is also a central straight avenue, a drive lined with huge plane trees.

Truly a park for people, Battersea Park offers something for all ages. Children have their own zoo, with furry things like otters, meerkats, guinea pigs and pygmy goats. For older people there is a bowling green. Those who are actively sporting are served by the new Millennium Arena, which offers indoor facilities for athletics, and there are tennis courts, cricket nets and football pitches. More fun can be had by cycling and roller skating along the drives or boating on the lake. Culture is catered for too: the old Victorian Pump House has been turned into a successful gallery, and the circus, ballet and theatre are also regular visitors. So too are large clusters of joyful dogs being exercised in the park by volunteers who help the famous Battersea Dogs Home.

For the Festival of Britain in 1951, the park became the site for the Festival Pleasure Gardens. The layout, inspired by the Tivoli

Gardens of Copenhagen, was designed with consciously modern style, ornamented by John Piper and Osbert Lancaster designs of fantasy buildings. Gardens included one by Russell Page. A funfair, cameo stalls, shops, water gardens, fountains, concert pavilion, restaurants and beer garden were featured. Colour in daytime and light at night were used with carnival panache to chase away the drabness of the recent war years. The zoo was improved and a tree walk built. It was all a huge success and the life of the Festival Gardens was extended for a further six months.

The park is large, nearly 200 acres, and there are quiet spaces beneath a collection of trees which includes a black Italian poplar (*Populus nigra*), the Kentucky coffee tree (*Gymnocladus dioica*), Chinese privet (*Ligustrum lucidum*) and a foxglove tree (*Paulownia tomentosa*) from Asia, plus a magnificent walnut (*Juglans nigra*), weeping birch (*Betula pendula* 'Youngii'), flowering horse chestnuts (*Aesculus indica*) and honey locusts (*Gleditsia triacanthos*). The enclosed Old English Garden was built in 1912 with timber pergolas for roses, wisteria and honeysuckle, below which are boxed beds with lavender, potentillas and flowering perennials. Seats, backed by yew hedges, surround a central classical pool. Another gardening area is the Battersea Garden Project. This is a hive of horticulture, run by Thrive, a national charity whose aim is to help disadvantaged and disabled people to enjoy the social activity of shared gardening. Close by is a wilderness that is classified as a nature reserve.

A striking change came about in 1985 when the Peace Pagoda was built beside the river. A gift to Londoners from a Buddhist order, it has four gilded Buddhas. The pagoda is lovingly cared for by a monk who resides in the park. Soon it will become part of the dramatic restoration plans for the park that are well under way at the time of writing. Sir James

Left Looking across the Thames to the gilded Peace Pagoda, now one of the landmarks on the south bank of the river.

Pennethorne's designs are being followed and the Embankment side of the park is nearly complete, as is the renewed subtropical garden and the rose garden.

WIMBLEDON COMMON
SW19

Undulating native woodland, grassland and heath cover this largest of all London commons. With wide skies, rambling ground and a wild nature, the common is inviting to the population of south-west London. And the history of the area makes its conservation as remarkable as that of Richmond Park and Hampstead Heath.

There are some archaeological traces, such as the Iron Age hill fort known misleadingly as Caesar's Camp, but actually dating to the fifth century BC. Later the lands were part of the Manor of Wimbledon. Tenants had some grazing rights and firewood could be taken in limited quantity. As common land it offered a venue for crowd-pulling fairs, shows, racing, troop exercises and parades. In the mid-eighteenth century, George III held stirring reviews on the commons. It also has a colourful history of highwaymen and duellists.

However, because the 'commoners' were tenants, 'common rights' were applied loosely and could be withdrawn. As the number of commoners dwindled and their rights fell into abeyance, the lord could enclose more and more of his land. In 1864, the Lord of the Manors of Wimbledon and Battersea, Earl Spencer, introduced to Parliament a bill that if passed would have enabled him to enclose 700 acres for himself and sell off 300 acres for development. Fortunately, after its second reading the bill went before a select committee, who had access to a report on London's commons and ensured that the bill was

Right Once there were many windmills on the high land around London. The famous Dutch windmill on Wimbledon Common is one of the few that still survives.

withdrawn. Eventually the Wimbledon and Putney Commons Act, passed in 1871, assured the preservation in perpetuity of both Wimbledon Common and nearby Putney Heath. Thus, as was so often the case, it was the Victorians who saved the land for the public. The site passed to a body of conservators, whose responsibilities were to retain it for public use and to care for the land. During both wars, Wimbledon Common and Putney Heath were used as army camps and some trenches can still be seen.

Today the common offers a multitude of functions. Areas are set aside for many different sports, for families who picnic or fly kites, for those who ride horses or bikes, for cross-country runners or metal detectors. The demands on the common are multifarious and everyone feels they have a legitimate right to use it. But many of the activities may interfere with the pleasures of those who value wildlife, as well as the continuing scientific research that takes place there. It is a tricky act to balance. Conservation has a major role and the conservators practise a deliberate policy of non-interference with nature, aiming to foster the common as ecologically rich areas. Minimal management means not no management but skilful understanding and anticipation of problems.

Visitors relish the wildlife, which includes rare wild flowers, heather, gorse and broom. There are badgers, foxes and over eighty-six species of birds thriving so close to London. An information centre can be found behind the windmill. Native plants have done well on the different soils and conditions. London clay underscores everything, laid down in Eocene times almost fifty-four million years ago; and the gravels and Bagshot sands that overlie it are the remnants of the terraces of the Thames valley. Now there are four main habitats. Three are natural: deciduous woodland on the western slopes of clay-based soil; gravelled plateaux of acid heathland, with gorse and broom growing on the sandy slopes; and boggy areas fed by acidic springs, where creeping willow, goat willow and sallow can be seen. A lot of open grassland that was once grazed now hosts bramble and dog roses. Other trees and shrubs include hazels, silver birch, hawthorn, blackthorn and holly, which have spread around the whole site.

The fourth habitat is the man-made gravel pits, now dammed and flooded. There are four ponds which create different habitats including areas of sphagnum bog. They are designated as Sites of Special Scientific Interest. Wildlife thrives, although there are problems now with invasive alien pond plants, including water fern (*Azolla filiculoides*), floating pennywort (*Hydrocotyle ranunculoides*) from the United States and Australian parrot's feather (*Myriophyllum aquaticum*). Possibly gardeners took the excess from their ornamental ponds and threw them into the wild pools, unaware of the damage they cause. Some are very dangerous because they cover the water surface with a continuous textured green, looking like grass and inviting little feet to explore. Apart from this, though, these plants destroy native plants like water lilies and bogbean, and are a menace to underwater life.

There have been windmills on the hills of the common since the seventeenth century. The one we see today was built in 1817 and is more like the windmills of Holland than those traditional in England. After major restoration it was opened as an interesting museum in 1976.

CANNIZARO PARK
SW19

Adding to the riches of Wimbledon Common is a large park on its west side. This was once the landscaped grounds of elegant Cannizaro House, a reproduction of an early eighteenth-century mansion that stood on the site but was burned down. The house is now a gracious hotel, but the park is owned by Merton Borough Council, which maintains this treasure to a very high standard.

From the heights of the house a rolling lawn sweeps downhill towards a richly profiled boundary of tree shapes, planted over the decades of private ownership. The mature collection includes some unusual ones such as the New Zealand kowhai (*Sophora tetraptera*), Chilean firebush (*Embothrium coccineum*), pomegranate, loquat, mulberry, sassafras and cork oak, not to mention a glorious laburnum walk. The park offers much to the lover of garden flowers. Snowdrops and crocus welcome the new season. Magnolias, azaleas and camellias, underscored with heathers, follow through until the Rose Garden is in flower. This is the time too for superb summer bedding and it is so pleasing to see this really well maintained. In autumn Japanese acers and azaleas blaze with colour.

Beside the house is a large sunken garden and round the corner a compact old walled garden, now laid out to include two corner summerhouses and Arts and Crafts paving of the 1920s. In both gardens, spring bulbs are followed by immaculate bedding, carpeting the scene with colour. The plots are well thought out with a colour theme for each. In the year of writing one particularly successful scheme specialized in intense yellows, dominated by French marigolds in rust, orange, gold and lemon with layers of gamboge gazanias and central areas of primrose limoniums plus a dash of deep purple petunias. The walled area concentrated on the cool side of pink: bergenias and pelargoniums ruled alongside zinnias, ranging from cool crimsons to a warming tomato pink, and with inserts of dark violet verbenas.

There is a water garden, a wild garden, a formal rose garden and an azalea dell. A slightly odd 'Renaissance-Gothic' aviary houses budgerigars, and other sources of entertainment for children are performances by the Polka Theatre in the Italian Garden. Every year Wimbledon Art College stages a sculpture exhibition in the park.

Right A bold carpeting of zinnias at Cannizaro Park.

OTHER PARKS AND GARDENS

SALTER'S GARDEN
EC2

This small formal garden designed by David Hicks is part of the Barbican complex. Ordered and symmetrical, the garden comprises a wide strip of mown grass bisected by paths and tunnels of honeysuckle. In summer the beds are fragrant with honeysuckle and roses.

ALBION SQUARE
E8

The Italianate design of this narrow rectangular garden, built in 1846–9 by Islip Odell, is elgantly simple. Lines of pollarded lime trees frame the long sides. At either end paths encircle identical beds that are planted with low, wide-spreading red-leaved trees, *Prunus* 'Pissardii Nigra'.

ST PETER'S SQUARE
W6

This charming Hammersmith square is distinguished by its surroundings. The stucco houses have pediments and Ionic porches ornamented by towering eagles and couchant lions. Many are further adorned with old wisterias that drape along the house fronts.

CARLYLE'S HOUSE
SW3

The simple rectangular garden of Thomas Carlyle's house at 24 Cheyne Row is walled and secluded. One wall at the far end survives from Tudor times, being a relic of the large garden of Shrewsbury House. The planting is Victorian and includes a large walnut, figs, vines, ferns and herbaceous beds, all box-edged. In this garden, Carlyle wrote, 'I can wander about in dressing gown and straw hat and take my pipe in peace.'

ST GEORGE'S FIELDS
W2

St George's Fields is known locally as the 'Hanging gardens of Bayswater' because of the luxuriance of trailing plants that cloaks the 1970s architecture. The layout of the flats follows the same principle of allowing room for plants as well as people, for there are garden spaces inside and around the linked buildings. Spacious enclosed lawns, mown in fluid curvaceous lines, are bordered by voluptuous planting that includes mature flowering shrubs and large mounds of clipped privet.

RAVENSCOURT PARK
W6

Ravenscourt has all the usual park areas set aside for children and sports, but many visitors find the Old English Scented Garden, set out for the visually impaired, its most attractive feature. The way the crazy paving has been laid, and the apparent flimsiness of the pergola give it a rather faded 1950s air. But though the pergola looks too frail to support the increasing weight of maturing rambling roses, wisteria, jasmine, passion flowers and solanum, the plants flourish and the vivid pink roses are extremely generous in their flowering.

Among other gardens of note are the fifteenth-century garden of Clothworkers' Hall in Mincing Lane, which survived the Great Fire; the popular West Ham Park, remarkable for its heritage as a botanic garden and for its roses, rock garden and many fine trees and shrubs; the contemplative Tibetan Peace Garden in Lambeth; the gentle Lanning Roper Memorial Garden at Trinity Hospice, near Clapham Common, which has romantic flows of perennials, a wild area and interesting sculpture; the Welsh Harp reservoir in Wembley, a Site of Special Scientific Interest, with wide open spaces; the intimate nature sites of Gillespie Park in Arsenal; St Mary Magdalen churchyard in East Ham; Hither Green Nature Reserve in Lewisham; and the tiny woodland reserve of Greville Place in Maida Vale. There are other nature reserves all over London, as at Totteridge Fields in Barnet, the Centre for Wildlife Gardening in Peckham and the Chase in Dagenham. Inner London also has Cable Street in the East End, the Phoenix Garden in the West End and St Mary's near Old Street. This last is run by the charity Thrive and is based upon active participation by disadvantaged people. There are also city farms. such as the old Mudchute Farm in East London, still a working farm, and the more recent Freightliners Farm in Holloway with its fruit trees and herbs. Here urban children are introduced to rural delights and, to some extent, realities.

LOST GARDENS

I owe it to history to acknowledge some of London's lost gardens. Some were small, like Myatt's Fields in Clerkenwell, named for the market gardener who grew strawberries here in the eighteenth century. No physical remains exist of Mulberry Garden, also in Clerkenwell, once very fashionable and opened every evening in 1742. On a grander scale were the elaborate gardens of Richmond Palace in Henry VII's day and the expansive gardens of Henry VIII's Nonsuch Palace in Streatham – all now vanished. In the seventeenth and eighteenth centuries it would have been unthinkable that the famed New Spring Garden at Vauxhall, a place for the demi-monde, for assemblies and masquerades, for balls, ballooning and fireworks, with a murky reputation as well, could vanish so completely. The Chinese pavilions, fountains, cascades, flowers, trees and trellises – all gone. But the enterprise of the past is still part of the beating heart of London.

USEFUL INFORMATION ABOUT PARKS AND GARDENS TO VISIT

Wild About Town is a pamphlet that lists many sites all over London. It can be obtained from the London Wildlife Trust, 47–51 Great Suffolk Street, London SE1 0BS.

In and Around London is a free informative booklet published by the National Trust, which includes gardens as well as houses that are open to the public. To obtain a copy, write to PO Box 39, Bromley, Kent BR1 3XL or e-mail enquiries@thenationaltrust.org.uk.

English Heritage owns 400 properties, including some in London. Opening arrangements can be found in the members' handbook or on the organization's website, www.english-heritage.org.uk. Guidebooks are available on site. For membership, contact Membership Department PO Box 570, Swindon SN2 2YR. Some sites can be visited free of charge and all are free to members.

Gardens of England and Wales Open for Charity, more familiarly known as the Yellow Book, is revised annually by the National Gardens Scheme. It describes private gardens that are open to the public on certain days. There is normally a small entrance charge that goes to charities. The book is available at most bookshops. For information, telephone 01483 211537 or visit the scheme's website, www.ngs.org.uk.

London Garden Squares Day is a leaflet produced annually by the London Historic Parks and Gardens Trust. To obtain a copy, send a stamped addressed envelope to LHPGT, Duck Island Cottage, St James's Park, London SW1A 2BJ.

The Museum of Garden History at Lambeth Palace Road, London SE1 7LB is mostly London orientated, but also a source of interest for those who take pleasure in all aspects of garden making. For information, and details of membership, telephone 020 7401 8865 or e-mail info@museumgardenhistory.org.uk.

The Royal Horticultural Society is the leading garden charity in England, known for its horticultural expertise, educational activities and publications. For details about membership, which includes free access to the Society's gardens and the famous shows, telephone 0845 130 4646 or visit the Society's website, www.rhs.org.uk.

FURTHER READING

Of the many books on London, the following are just a few that I found useful.

Lorna Lister, *Exploring London's Gardens, a Seasonal Guide*, self-published, 2001. Highly accessible.

Andrew Crowe, *The Parks and Woodlands of London*, Fourth Estate, 1987. A comprehensive and very readable guide that includes easily followed maps.

Todd Longstaffe-Gowan, *The London Town Garden 1740–1840*, Yale University Press, 2001. Thorough and fascinating.

Ben Weinreb and Christopher Hibbert, eds, *The London Encyclopaedia*, 1995, Macmillan. Invaluable, informative and hefty.

Andrew Gumbel, *London*, Cadogan, 2000. Witty and discerning.

David McDowall and Deborah Wolton, *Hampstead Heath: the Walker's Guide*, David McDowall, 1998. Provides much of local interest for ramblers.

Geoffrey Young, *Walking London's Parks and Garden*, New Holland, 1998. A very informative read, full of fascinating detail; with maps.

Hunter Davies, *A Walk Round London's Parks*, Hamish Hamilton, 1983. Highly personal and peppered with anecdotal chat, making it a good, informative read.

Nature Areas for City People and *Ecology and Nature Conservation in London*: part of an interesting series of books produced by the London Ecology Unit, Bedford House, 125 Camden High Street, NW1 7JR.

I am very grateful to the Garden History Society, whose scholarly manuals have been sources of information. For people interested in the historical and contemporary gardens of Britain and elsewhere, membership of this unique society is rewarding. Contact the Membership Secretary, Garden History Society, 70 Crowcross Street, London EC1M 6EJ.

Right Shooting fireworks light up the sky over London.

INDEX
References to main entries are shown in bold type, those to illustration captions in italics.

ACKNOWLEDGMENTS

Author's acknowledgments

Sandra Lousada and I spent many happy hours together, discovering and relishing the parks and gardens in this book. I must thank her for her superb, revealing photography, and for her energy, drive, sensitivity and above all humour, which have made this such a happy year.

I am grateful to Frances Lincoln for giving me the chance to work on such an enjoyable book and deeply regret that she did not live to see it completed. I appreciate the great interest shown by the editors, Jo Christian and Anne Askwith; and by the art editor, Anne Fraser, who, with perceptive insight and gentle encouragement, has followed through her passion for the subject, constantly nurturing our own enthusiasm. I would also like to thank Bernard Williams of the Worshipful Company of Gardeners for his help and the Edmonton Hundred Historical Society for access to its research papers.

Photographer's acknowledgments

A million thanks to Jo Christian and Anne Fraser for giving me the chance to work on a subject entirely new to me. Their support was continuous and encouraging. It has been a very interesting project, to see how Londoners use their green spaces. Working with Jill Billington has been the icing on the cake. Without her enthusiastic guidance I would not have known where to begin; she has fired me with interest in a new subject and I thoroughly enjoyed working with her. Lastly thanks to my husband, Brian Richards, for devoting so much time to walking the parks with me. It was wonderful to have his support and architectural eye.

And many thanks to the following people for their help: Joanne Smith at the Camley Street Project; Lin Skippings at Carlyle's House; Rosie Atkins, Christopher Leach and Maureen O'Brady at Chelsea Physic Garden; Simon Haines and Paul Pollard at Clifton Nurseries; Isabelle Evans and Kate Knowles at Dulwich Art Gallery; Jane Cordingley and Christine Grey at Eltham Palace; Jane Ellis at Fenton House; Nancy Loder of the Geffrye Museum; Christine Guthrie at Ham House; Rachel Whitburn at Hampton Court; Jean Pateman, Friends of Highgate Cemetery (chairman); Luke Hull at Kew; Anne Jennings at the Museum of Garden History, Lambeth Palace; Siobhan Scullion at Osterley; David Best at No. 1 Poultry; Victoria Ainsworth at the Roof Garden, Kensington; David Perkins of Roots and Shoots; Martin Senior at the Wetlands, Barnes.